Walter Fitz Patrick

The Great Condé and the Period of the Fronde

Vol. 1

Walter Fitz Patrick

The Great Condé and the Period of the Fronde
Vol. 1

ISBN/EAN: 9783337396350

Printed in Europe, USA, Canada, Australia, Japan

Cover: Foto ©ninafisch / pixelio.de

More available books at **www.hansebooks.com**

THE GREAT CONDÉ

AND

THE PERIOD OF THE FRONDE.

A HISTORICAL SKETCH.

BY

WALTER FITZ PATRICK.

VOL. I.

London:
T. CAUTLEY NEWBY, PUBLISHER,
30, WELBECK STREET, CAVENDISH SQUARE.
1873.

THE GREAT CONDÉ AND THE PERIOD OF THE FRONDE.

CHAPTER I.

THE House of Bourbon is descended from a younger son of St. Louis. Charles of Bourbon, Duke of Vendôme, who died in the year 1536, left three sons—Anthony, Duke of Vendome, who by his marriage with Jeanne d'Albret became King of Navarre; the Cardinal of Bourbon, whom the Catholic League afterwards proclaimed King of France in opposition to his nephew, Henry IV.; and Louis, first Prince of Condé. Louis embraced the reformed tenets, and was the leader of the Huguenot party in the religious troubles which broke out in France after the death of Henry II. He was an ambitious and turbulent prince of great courage and some capacity, but his fortunes paled

before the splendid genius of Francis Duke of
Guise. He was about to be led to the block in
1559, when the sudden death of King Francis II.,
throwing the reins of government into the hands
of the Queen-mother, Catherine de Medici, gave
him life and liberty. In 1562 he was defeated
and taken prisoner by Guise at the battle of
Dreux. After the assassination of the Great
Duke by Palliot, an emissary of Admiral Coligni,
while he was besieging Orleans in the following
year, Condé again recovered his freedom, and held
a leading position in the State until he was defeated and killed at the battle of Jarnac in 1569.

The son of Louis, Henry, second Prince of
Condé, was brought up in his father's faith, in
intimate association with Jeanne d'Albret, and
her son, the young Prince of Bearn, who succeeded
to the kingdom of Navarre at his mother's death
in 1572. Henry of Condé shared the fortunes of
his cousin after the massacre of St. Bartholomew,
and during the early part of the wars of the
League. He especially distinguished himself at
the battle of Courtias in 1587. A few months
after this victory he died at St. Jean d'Angely.
The circumstances surrounding his death excited
strong suspicion of foul play on the part of his
wife Charlotte, daughter of the Duke of la Tremouille. She was accused of poisoning her hus-

band in order to prevent his discovering her adultery with a page named Belcastel, of which her condition was likely to afford conclusive evidence; and after a trial on this charge before a Huguenot tribunal at St. Jean d'Angely, was condemned to death. Being with child, she was respited pending her accouchement, and imprisoned in a tower of the town, where later in the year she gave birth to a son. In the meantime the Parliament of Paris, claiming exclusive jurisdiction over criminals of her rank, declared the sentence of death invalid on account of the incompetency of the court, and, as on the death of Henry III. in the same year the acknowledged princes of the blood, the Prince of Conti, the Count of Soissons, and the Cardinal of Bourbon, were Catholics; the Huguenots, reluctant to injure the claims of the princess's child as next heir to his cousin, Henry IV., allowed the judgment to remain dormant. The princess, however, remained a prisoner till 1595, when Henry IV., firmly seated on the French throne, feeling dissatisfied at the turbulent proceedings of the Court of Soissons, annulled the sentence of death. Although Henry had made no secret of his own conviction of her guilt, he granted Madame de Condé a new trial before the Parliament of Paris. The High Court declared her innocent, whereupon the King acknowledged her son as first Prince of the blood, and caused him to be educated at St. Germain in the Catholic Faith.

The 16th century undoubtedly forms one of the most important epochs in the history of the world. Never, at any other period, has the human mind been more deeply stirred by questions of more tremendous moment; no other period has produced a greater number of extraordinary characters. But exactly in proportion to the vehemence of the strife which convulsed the leading nations of Europe, its passions, noble and ignoble, warped and clouded men's minds, and prevented their always estimating justly the characters of their leaders. The gods of the popular worship, as seen through the turbid haze of party enthusiasm, enthroned on lofty pinnacles, and radiant with undying glory, occasionally prove, in the clear atmosphere of historical truth, mean and grovelling idols, having fronts of brass and feet of clay. With perhaps one exception, there is no public character of great mark that bears worse the strong light which modern research has thrown upon the 16th century than Henri Quatre, to whom flatterers have given the much-abused title of The Great. The exception is Queen Elizabeth of England, whose real character is so vividly presented to us in the confidential correspondence of the singularly able and crooked statesmen, who, in their own interests, propped her throne, and were the sport and the victims of her cunning hypocrisy and capricious humours. Vain, false, cruel, crafty, inconstant, and sordidly avaricious, joining much that is most repulsive in the rioting passions of a fierce and gross masculine nature to the most unloveable failings of her own sex— the coarse ferocity and ruthless temper of Henry VIII., to the fickle selfishness of a coquette, and the caressing guile of a tigress—these traits of Elizabeth's character are apparent, even from the reluctant evidence of modern historians of her own party. But we find scarcely a trace of the glorious intellect, not a glimpse of the greatness of soul, which popular fancy has attributed to the last of the Tudor sovereigns.

In truth, Henry's claims to the lofty titles which sectarian prejudice and national vanity have lavished on him rest on as slender foundations. He had the restless energy, the buoyant spirit, and the brilliant—if somewhat boastful—courage characteristic of the Gascons, with a sagacious sense and a strong love of his own interests, unclouded and unfettered by any motive or restraint, except the ephemeral chains woven by an insatiable propensity to gallantry. He had a pleasant wit, frank and familiar manners, not always free from deceit, and, when his interests or his passions did not arouse what was tyrannical in his disposition, an easy good nature, which was prone to degenerate into weakness. What perhaps has contributed most to his wide popularity is the saying attributed to him, that he wished every French peasant to have a fowl boiling in his pot. This is one of those sounding sentiments of visionary benevolence which captivate the minds of men, especially of Frenchmen; and which, if it had expressed in any degree the policy of their ruler, would have entitled him to the gratitude of his subjects. But it was merely a gush of cheap philanthropy which he exemplified by loading his impoverished kingdom, desolated by the wars of the League, with excessive taxation, in order to extort the means of indulging his costly vices, and of plunging unwilling Europe, without any just pretext, into a desperate conflict, an earlier unchaining of the fiendish passions and the unutterable woes of the Thirty Years' War.

But circumstances were singularly favourable to Henri Quatre. The last three kings of the house of Valois, his predecessors and contemporaries, were among the least estimable of French sovereigns. The brilliant sceptre of Francis I. had descended to the vile brood of Catherine of Medicis, the sickly and feeble-minded

Francis II.; Charles IX., whose brief and unhappy life was a restless condition of morbid self-torture, passing at intervals from the sullen frenzy of brooding suspicion to the wild frenzy of unbridled rage; Henry III., the most infamous of mankind.

Before Henry IV. was entitled to claim the succession to the French crown, the family of Lorraine-Guise, the most illustrious on the splendid roll of French nobility—perhaps the most illustrious in modern annals—which had furnished two generations of champions and martyrs to the Catholic cause, the grand figures of the men towering above a race of giants, the women peerless in beauty, in cultivated intellect, and in the noble fortitude that vanquishes misfortune, had been robbed of its strength and its glory by the hands of assassins. A branch of the house of Lorraine, in comparison with which even the royal race of Capet was mean, the Guises traced back their august lineage through a long line of warrior princes to the Imperial figure of Charlemagne. By one of those strange revolutions which time brings about, the house of Lorraine, deriving its origin from the great Frank who re-established the Roman empire of the west— after many centuries of inferior, though not obscure, sovereignty—had risen again to the summit of greatness in three generations of

Roman Emperors, when the Imperial fabric crumbled beneath the sword of a conqueror greater even than Charlemagne. Francis, Duke of Guise is, by universal consent, one of the most splendid and stainless characters in history. He possessed in a superlative degree all the qualities that attract admiration and love, and his life was a noble example of public and private virtue. His six brothers stood in repute second only to him. The Cardinal of Lorraine, besides being renowned throughout Europe as a theologian and a scholar, was the most profound, vigorous, and accomplished statesman France has produced, with the exception of Cardinal Richelieu. Nor were the women of the family inferior to the men. For courage, capacity for government, virtue, and beauty, Mary, wife of James V. of Scotland, had no equal among the princesses of her time. The brilliant and engaging qualities, the ardent attachment to their faith, the deep mutual affection binding its members together in unwavering fidelity, the extraordinary majesty and beauty of person, worthy of its Imperial origin and Imperial spirit, that distinguished the entire family, gave it an indisputable pre-eminence which is recognised with an admiration rising to wonder in the diplomatic correspondence of the period.

The son of Francis, Henry Duke of Guise, if of

a character less lofty and pure than his heroic father, rivalled him in military and political genius, in the strength of his religious convictions, and in the splendour of his personal gifts. It is in reference to him that the Duchess of Retz, the most accomplished and fastidious lady of the court of Catherine of Medicis, and by no means a partial critic, says, " Those princes of the house of Lorraine have so noble and majestic a mien that in comparison to them, all other men appear plebeian and common." But when Henry of Guise fell in the hour of his triumph, perfidiously murdered by Henry II., as his father had been cut off in his career of victory by an assassin suborned by Coligni, the house of Lorraine-Guise and the Catholic cause fell under the leadership of the self-seeking and sluggish Mayenne. To Mayenne Henri Quatre was as superior as he was inferior to either Duke of Guise. At the very beginning of the struggle between them, when the chances of success seemed decidedly on the side of the Catholic League, Pope Sixtus V. said that the Bearnais must win, because he spent less time in bed than Mayenne did at his meals. In fact, when Henry had once made up his mind to conform to the Catholic faith, the issue of the conflict was no longer doubtful. And when France had again become united, and the religious passions of the time began to cool down, the religious element which had been the essential feature of the Civil War was gradually lost sight of, or purposely disregarded in favour of the political element which had been an accident. The old national spirit of rivalry to Spain, which had been overpowered for a time by a still stronger sentiment, revived in all its former intensity. The ex-Huguenot leader was forgotten in the gallant king who had freed France from the domination of Philip II. National vanity, personified in later times by Voltaire, has invested the only sovereign of the disastrous period of French history that followed the death of Henry II.—whose character or capacity was not contemptible—with all the qualities that should adorn a sage and a hero.

Whether we regard Henry IV. from an intellectual or a moral point of view, his claims to greatness do not bear investigation. His talents as a ruler were not more than respectable. In the beginning of his reign, when his council was composed of men of but ordinary ability, and not always of ordinary integrity, his affairs fell into a state of frightful confusion, with which he was utterly unable of himself to grapple. It was only when he virtually surrendered the two great departments of the administration to two very able men—Villeroy, the most expert of politicians;

and Sully, stern, frugal, and unscrupulous, whose one rule of conduct was devotion to the interests of his master—that his government exhibited skill in diplomacy, or order in finance. And the most anxious cares of Sully were caused by the unkingly follies and caprices that constantly thwarted the great minister's labours.

The military talents of Henry were not of a high order. It is true that he won great renown as the victor at Arques and Ivry. And so far as the heroic spirit of a leader determines the fate of battles, he deserved his renown. But, besides that, whatever of warlike skill existed at the time in France, and perhaps at no period was French generalship at so low an ebb, had enlisted under the royal banner, Henry had on his side the sloth, the indecision, and the incapacity of his opponent, Mayenne. When pitted against the Duke of Parma, the contrast between the royal "Captain of Horse" and the consummate Spanish general was ludicrous. The ease with which the great master of war, although sinking under a mortal illness, twice led his small army from the Netherlands into the heart of France, baffling with the calm contempt of superior science every effort of the French King to retard his movements or compel him to fight, and, without a blow, raising the sieges of Rouen and Paris; his astonishing feat of carrying his troops, which, during one of the paroxysms of his disorder, had been shut up without supplies and without apparent possibility of escape, in an angle of the Seine, near Rouen, across the broad and rapid river, in the face of his amazed foes, without the loss of a single man or a single gun; and the deliberate skill with which, when he had accomplished his objects, he slowly marched back again into Flanders, the whole chivalry of the kingdom following on his track in helpless rage and mortification, inflicted greater humiliation on the French arms than the loss of two pitched battles.

The moral character of Henry was despicable. The facility with which he changed his belief, as if it was merely a garment, outraged even the lax public morality of that age. The more distinguished leaders of the Protestant party throughout Europe, however eminent for parts and for force of will, were not, as a rule, influenced by deep religious convictions. As in the case of Maurice of Saxony, probably the ablest of them all, their religion was a part of their policy. They were statesmen who regarded the vehement theological ferment, that stirred in the minds of their followers, as a vigorous power, which, if skilfully directed, might achieve empire. But though for the greater part unencumbered with scruples,

they generally maintained in their outer conduct
a decent show of conformity to the opinions and
feelings of their adherents. Henry, however,
with a cynical levity peculiar to himself, habitually
adapted his creed to his interests. And to this
shameless disregard of obligations, the most
sacred amongst men, which enabled him to take
full advantage of the sentiment of hereditary
right, so strongly cherished by Frenchmen at that
time, he owed his success, far more than to his
political or military abilities. When established
on the throne, his personal conduct as a ruler was
seldom shaped in consonance with any standard
of high principle or enlightened statesmanship.
When he was not tyrannical he was weak. He
was always selfish. The most sacred motives of
justice and of honour, the longest and most brilliant services, weighed as nothing in his mind in
comparison with the policy or inclination of the
moment. He was easily moved to tears, to bursts
of hysterical emotion at a grief that touched himself. He would weep piteously in recounting
what he suffered from some ludicrous freak of a
coquettish mistress. But he was incapable alike
of large-minded benevolence, or of a generous
and lasting attachment.

With the exception of the old Marshal Biron,
who had died for his cause, no one had done more

to seat him on the throne than the Marshal's son, the Duke of Biron. They had long been sworn comrades and brothers-in-arms. Biron was vain and irritable. Rightly or wrongly, he entertained the belief that his services had not been sufficiently recompensed; that others less deserving had been preferred to himself. Smarting under a sense of injustice, he gave ear to the perfidious counsels of a secretary, and while commanding an army against the Duke of Savoy, allowed himself to be drawn into a treasonable correspondence with the enemies of France. The negotiations, however, were still incomplete when he was struck with remorse, and, repairing to Lyons, confessed his treason to the King. Henry, taken by surprise, fell on his old friend's neck in a passion of tears, and granted him full pardon. After the termination of the war, Biron, who had retired to his government of Burgundy, received an invitation from the King to repair to Fontainebleau. The missive contained the royal pledge that no harm should befal him. The Duke, contrary to the advice of his friends, went up to Court. He was received by Henry with a gush of tender affection, but after a few days, during which his movements were closely watched, he was suddenly arrested, and despite of pardon and pledge, was arraigned before the Parlia-

ment of Paris for the crime which had been
condoned at Lyons, sentenced to death, and beheaded on the Place de Grève. It is true that
Henry, who was keenly sensitive to the horror
which this tyrannical act provoked throughout
Europe, and to the feelings of indignation and
distrust which it aroused in the French nobility,
afterwards alleged, in his own justification, that
proofs of new treasons on the part of Biron had
come to light, and that the Duke's obstinacy in
refusing to confess his guilt was the sole cause of
his ruin. But Biron was entrapped by means of
a formal pledge of safety sent to him by his
sovereign when in full possession of all the evidence. He denied to his last breath the additional
accusations, which rested on the unsupported
testimony of his secretary and tempter, a man of
infamous character, who had been bought, if not
suborned, by the Duke of Sully. And the only
really weighty charge preferred against the Duke
at his trial, that which determined the judgment of
the High Court, related to the acts which he did not
deny, and for which he pleaded his sovereign's
pardon. Unfortunately for himself, in his reliance
on the King's faith, he had scorned the prudent
advice of the Constable Montmorenci to demand
an official pardon under the Great Seal, which
could have been produced in evidence; and the

remorseless policy of Sully, which, aimed by a terrible example to strike dismay into the haughty and turbulent nobles who treated him with open disdain, worked on the jealous fears of Henry, and rendered Biron's confidence in his master fatal to himself.

Many other well-known incidents of his reign indicated, though in a less tragical way, how greatly, where the claims of past service and tried friendship clashed with a present purpose, Henry was prone to the ignoble vice of ingratitude.

But it is in his relations with the fairer half of his subjects which formed not the least important feature in the history of his reign, and brought him into disgraceful collision with his young kinsman, the Prince of Condé, that the true character of this king is most clearly seen. In truth, it is difficult to conceive two human beings more essentially different than the Henri Quatre of Romance, the soul of chivalry, the wise and magnanimous sovereign, the idol of the brave and the fair, and the Henri Quatre, mean-spirited, tyrannical, jealous, infatuated, supremely ridiculous, who has been sketched by the friendly pens of Sully, the Princess of Conti, Bassompierre, and others, among his most intimate associates. The slave of his passion for the sex, he seems never to have succeeded in gaining the love or respect of a woman. It is not easy to say whether his marriages or his liaisons reflect more discredit on himself, or were more prolific of troubles to the State.

His first wife, the beautiful and accomplished Margaret of Valois, had been deeply attached in early life to Henry, Duke of Guise. Charles IX., her brother, incited to a frantic jealousy of his great subject by the arts of her second brother, the Duke of Anjou, threatened to kill Guise with his own hand if he persisted in a suit in which his affections were engaged; and is said to have resorted to personal violence to compel his sister to a union which she loathed. Despising and detesting a husband who took her for political convenience, and then in order to secure freedom in the pursuit of his pleasures, accorded her similar liberty of conduct, Margaret abandoned herself to shameless excesses. The marriage, irregular in itself, and endured with repugnance, proved unfruitful. Henry afterwards wrung from Margaret, when her kindred were all dead, and her friends alienated by her misconduct, a consent to a divorce, by threatening her with a public trial for the profligacy at which he had connived.

His second wife, Mary of Medicis, was a woman of high spirit and quick temper. The open insults passed on her by her husband and his imperious mistress, the Marchioness of Verneuil, who publicly challenged the validity of her marriage, provoked her beyond endurance. The Court was torn by angry contentions. Domestic grievances generated dangerous political cabals, and the almost daily task of allaying the mutual animosities of the king, his wife and his mistress, severely taxed the patience and skill of Sully. Sounds of recrimination and violence frequently burst from the royal apartments. On one occasion Henry rushed undressed from his wife's bedchamber to complain to Sully that she had struck him in the face, and to concert measures with his minister for obtaining another divorce. So notorious were the quarrels of the royal pair, that on the assassination of the King, the crime was popularly attributed to the joint contrivance of Mary of Medicis and her former rival, the Marchioness of Verneuil, whom common thirst for revenge was supposed to have united for his destruction.

The lives of Henriette de Balzac, Marchioness of Verneuil, and Gabrielle d'Estrées, Duchess of Beaufort, belong to history. Both regarded Henry with indifference; both were reluctantly induced to accept a disgraceful position under pressure of a scandalous abuse of the royal authority, tempered by distinct promises of marriage. Gabrielle loved and was betrothed to the hand-

some Duke of Bellegarde, one of the great
Catholic nobles who had remained faithful to
Henry III. and after that monarch's death, loyally
supported the Bearnais as legitimate king. Bellegarde, in the unreserved freedom of familiar
intercourse, indiscreetly boasted to his sovereign
and friend of Gabrielle's unrivalled beauty; and
as Henry affected scepticism on the subject, invited him to come and see her. Henry came, saw,
and was conquered. He immediately forbade the
marriage; exiled the Duke, silenced the remonstrances of the lady's friends with threats of
vengeance, and by every ungenerous and every
unholy means which profligacy could suggest or
arbitrary power compass, compelled her to consent
to his wishes. She bore her chains for years,
doing constant violence to her better nature and
her inclinations, in consequence of his pledges to
make her queen of France and legitimate her
children. If ever Henry entertained anything
approaching to genuine regard for a human being
it was for Gabrielle d'Estrées. Her death, after
horrible and protracted agonies, which seized
her at the end of a banquet given to her on
Thursday in Holy Week by the celebrated Zamet,
a low-born Italian protegé of Catherine of Medicis,
who, making the crimes and vices of the most
infamous court of modern Europe the stepping-

stones of his fortune, had risen to be the greatest usurer and pander of his time, seemed to overwhelm her lover with grief. Henry declared, in a touching epistle to his sister, which was stained with his tears, that his heart was for ever broken; that it lay buried in his mistress's tomb. But when Sully, immediately afterwards, suggested to him that Gabrielle's death released him from the embarrassing consequences of the frequent promises of marriage he had made to her, he at once became cheerful. All the circumstances attending Gabrielle's death pointed to a foul murder. She had repeatedly exclaimed, in piteous tones, that she was poisoned. Although in a dying state, she had insisted, with the desperate pertinacity of extreme terror, on being removed from Zamet's house. Yet Henry stifled all inquiry, continued his patronage to the ill-famed but convenient Italian, and, before three weeks had expired, was using all the resources of force and fraud to win the person of Henriette de Balzac.

Henriette was a clever and brilliant coquette. She knew that the King was on the point of obtaining from the Pope the long-sought-for annulment of his marriage with Margaret of Valois; and she aspired to be Queen of France. Her connexions were high and powerful; and, before she would accept Henry's proposals, she exacted from him a written promise, regularly attested, to make her his wife on condition that she bore him offspring within a year. She performed her part of the compact. He violated his without scruple; compelled the surrender of the compromising document by force; but was unable to prevent the outraged feelings of the lady and her kindred from raising up formidable troubles against his own peace and that of his kingdom during the remainder of his reign, or the shadow of illegitimacy from resting on his children by Mary of Medicis. The whole history of his relations with his two mistresses; his selfish tyranny; his doting weakness; the tricks they played him; their futile efforts to throw off a wearisome vassalage; his maudlin tears and his tragic airs; his ever restless jealousy, displaying itself now in mean espionage, now in acts of oppression towards suspected rivals; his total want of faith and honour; the incredible self-abasement with which he sacrificed his dignity as a man, and his duties as a sovereign, in vain efforts to propitiate his angry mistresses; even when softened down in the partial pages of his panegyrist Sully, would be infinitely amusing, if they did not form one of the most astonishing and humiliating pictures of human infirmity that the world has known.

But his conduct towards his young cousin, the Prince of Condé, stamps Henry's memory with even deeper dishonour. In the early part of the year 1609, there appeared at Court, in a ballet given by Mary of Medicis, a young lady, then about sixteen, of incomparable grace and beauty; Charlotte, youngest daughter of the Constable Montmorenci. The portraits of her that exist are disappointing; but it is clear from the enthusiastic description of Cardinal Bentivoglio, and other less grave chroniclers of that time, that nature had endowed her with extraordinary gifts of person and mind. The brilliancy of this new star dazzled the Court; and Henry, whose amorous temperament was unchilled by the frosts of nearly sixty winters, found his heart in a flame. Charlotte had been brought up in almost complete seclusion by her aunt, Diana of France, Duchess of Angouleme, at Vincennes; but the fame of her charms had spread abroad, and before she reached her thirteenth year, her father had been importuned with the most splendid offers for her hand. He had rejected them all curtly; but now, to the astonishment of every one, and of no one more than the fortunate object of his choice, he proposed her as a wife, with an enormous dower, to the Marquis of Bassompierre, the most brilliant of adventurers, whose attractive qualities had taken by storm the eccentric old Constable's heart.

Bassompierre was a cadet of a poor family of the second order of nobility in Lorraine; his father had been in the service of Henry, Duke of Guise. About ten years before this time, he had made his appearance at the Court of France, a stripling of twenty, without money or interest. But he was one of the handsomest and wittiest men of the age, adorned with all the graces and accomplishments of a perfect courtier—brave, amiable, and politic. His shining qualities soon won for him a distinguished place in the favour of the King, who made him the companion of all his parties of pleasure; and it is a strong testimony to his tact and prudence, that he was not less the favourite of Mary of Medicis. Without possessing any patrimony, he rivalled in magnificence and profusion the greatest nobles of the kingdom. The means of his extravagance were supplied chiefly by his extraordinary luck at play. He relates in his memoirs that at the ceremony of the baptism of the royal children in the year 1606, his dress cost fourteen thousand crowns, an enormous sum at that time. When he gave the order to his tailor his whole fortune amounted to seven hundred crowns, but by the end of a month he had won enough to pay for the habit, and to purchase a diamond-hilted sword, which completed his costume.

The King, seemingly over-joyed at the good fortune of his boon companion, at once assented to the marriage. But the connexions of the proud house of Montmorenci were furious, and conspired to break it off. Henry's passion for the young beauty was the talk of the whole Court, and they sought in the King's weakness the means of accomplishing their design. It was privately represented to him that the handsome, fascinating Bassompierre would infallibly win Charlotte's affections; that the contemplated union would be the death-blow of his own hopes. Before the day fixed for the nuptials, Henry, one morning before rising, summoned his favourite to his bedside. With abundance of sighs and tears, he confided to the astonished lover, as his dearest friend, his guilty designs upon this friend's affianced bride. In pathetic accents, he confessed his love for Charlotte, and his intention to reserve her to be the comfort and solace of his old age. He said that if the match proceeded, he and Bassompierre would be certain to quarrel; that he was resolved to introduce the young lady into his own family by giving her in marriage to the Prince of Condé, who, caring nothing for women, and devoting all his hours to the chase, would not be a bar to his happiness. The sudden clouding over of the splendid fortune which had dawned upon him, for a few moments overwhelmed Bassompierre with grief and despair. But he reflected that ineffectual opposition would only ruin all his prospects in life. Recovering himself quickly, he replied, with the best grace he could, that he had long passionately desired an opportunity of evincing his devotion and gratitude to his master; an adequate occasion now presented itself, and he gladly sacrificed all his happiness in life to promote his sovereign's felicity. Henry embraced the unfortunate courtier tenderly, and forthwith commanded the marriage of Mademoiselle de Montmorenci with the Prince of Condé.

The young Prince and the Constable both demurred. The former was of a very shy reserved temper, and was painfully sensitive regarding the cloud that rested on his birth. The King's notorious admiration of the young lady excited his distrust; but a threat of imprisonment in the Bastille frightened him into acquiescence. An income of one hundred thousand livres was settled on him by the Crown, and the marriage was celebrated at Chantilly. A few days afterwards, the Prince and his wife were ordered to appear at some Court festivities; and Henry, discarding all the restraints of decency, openly displayed his passion for the

Princess in the most extravagant fashion. He
indulged in such juvenile follies; he played such
fantastic pranks, decked out in scented collars and
gorgeous satin sleeves; he publicly raved in such
wild, incoherent raptures, that Charlotte fondly
believed his love for her had deprived him of
reason. Her husband, frantic with rage and
shame, ordered her to leave the Court; Henry
ordered her to remain. Then came scandalous
scenes of recrimination between the kinsmen, and
tyranny on the part of the King. He stopped
Condé's income, reproached him with the illegitimacy of his birth, and deliberated about shutting
him up in the Bastille.

At length, through the interference of the Constable, the Prince was able to remove his wife to
the Chateau of Muret in Picardy, and place her in
charge of his mother. Charlotte does not seem
to have entertained a very lively sense of gratitude for her husband's efforts in her behalf.
Henry had calculated rightly that the union was
not likely to be cemented by conjugal affection.
She was pleased by the admiration she excited, and
shuddered at the gloomy solitude of Muret, and
the uncongenial companionship of her mother-in-
law. Her royal adorer followed her in hot pursuit.
On St. Hubert's Day the two Princesses came
forth to witness a great hunt in honour of the

festival. Charlotte's attention was soon attracted by a *piqueur*, with a long beard and a large patch over one of his eyes, who was stationed at a little distance, with two dogs in a leash, and gazed upon her intently. A closer scrutiny enabled her to recognise the King under his disguise. The Princesses afterwards repaired for luncheon to a neighbouring chateau; and Henry, by the connivance of the hostess, feasted his eyes on the object of his adoration through a small hole cut in the tapestry of the saloon. He then rashly shifted his position to the window of an opposite apartment, and began gesticulating like a madman. But the Dowager Princess caught sight of him, carried off her charge in great indignation, and informed her son of the King's pursuit.

Condé saw that his only safety lay in immediate and secret flight from the kingdom. He pretended to his wife that he was about to return with her to court, for the accouchement of Mary of Medicis, in obedience to a royal summons; and, placing her, all joyful, in a coach, surrounded by his retainers, took the road to the Low Countries. The vehicle broke down on the journey; but Condé, allowing the princess scarcely a moment for repose, made her mount behind him on a pillion, and riding the whole of a wild November night through torrents of rain, succeeded in placing her,

c 2

half dead with cold and hunger, and devoured by chagrin, beyond the reach of his venerable rival.

The rapidity of his flight saved him from an unexpected danger. At the beginning of the journey the guide, suspecting its object, despatched his son in all haste to Paris to inform the King. The messenger arrived late.at night at the Louvre, while Henry was at play with some of his courtiers. When the news was whispered in his ear he started up in great agitation, and called Bassompierre aside. "*Mon ami,*" he said, "I am lost. Our man has lured his wife into a wood either to murder her or carry her off." He then rushed off to his wife's bedroom, and summoned all the ministers to attend him. Mary of Medicis had a few days before given birth to a daughter, and was still an invalid. When Sully arrived from the Arsenal, in very bad humour at the untimely disturbance of his slumbers, he found Henry pacing his wife's room with disordered air and incoherent mutterings, like a man distracted. The ministers stood in a row against the wall confounded and aghast, proffering contradictory counsels, all of which the King ordered to be immediately carried out. The poor Queen was looking on from her bed, a helpless spectator of a scene which was in itself one of the grossest outrages that could be offered to her. Henry, rushing up to Sully, told him what had happened, and was coolly upbraided by the virtuous and grim-visaged minister for not having shut up the Prince in the Bastille. Then orders were despatched to the garrisons on the Flemish frontier for the arrest of the fugitives; and so rapidly were these commands conveyed that Condé did not cross the frontier a moment too soon.

The Archduke Albert, son of the Emperor Maximilian II., and his wife Isabella, daughter of Philip II. of Spain, were at this time joint Sovereigns of the Low Countries. It was known to them that the French monarch had completed his formidable preparations for a war against the house of Austria; and therefore the appeal which the French Prince addressed to them for protection, on entering their dominions, was extremely embarrassing, as being likely to furnish a pretext for aggression. However, chiefly through the influence of Isabella, permission was accorded to Condé to place his wife under the charge of his brother-in-law, the Prince of Orange, at Brussels; and after some difficulty and delay he was allowed to repair thither himself. Henry sent de Praslin, the captain of his Guards, and afterwards the Marquis of Cœuvres, on special missions to the Flemish Court, to persuade his injured cousin to return with his wife; and in case of refusal, to proclaim him a traitor, and require the surrender of the exiles from the Archduke under threat of war. Condé, proving deaf to solicitation and menace, Cœuvres demanded an audience of the Flemish Sovereigns, and insisted in peremptory terms that the Princess at least should be delivered up to him. The Archduke Albert politely excused himself from separating a wife from her husband; but the spirit of Isabella the Catholic, flashed out in the response of the Archduchess. "I think," she said, " such a demand a very ludicrous and unusual article in the instructions of an ambassador. I am a Spanish woman, and do not deem myself obliged to act as pander to the unrighteous passions of your King." Without waiting for a reply she turned her back on the rebuked Cœuvres, and left the room. The French envoy then, with the connivance of the young Princess, arranged a plan for carrying her off from the Hotel of the Prince of Orange. The plot was skilfully contrived, and would probably have succeeded had it not been betrayed by Mary of Medicis to the Flemish Embassy at Paris. The result was that the Archduchess, under pretext of doing honour to her guest, invited her to take up her abode in the Royal Palace, and assigned her apartments adjoining her own. The grief, and mortification of Madame de Condé were great.

Henry was frantic. He had Condé attainted and sentenced to death as a traitor by the Parliament of Paris. He wrote with his own hand intemperate despatches to his representatives at foreign Courts, in which, to the especial amusement of his own subjects, he expatiated in the bitterest terms on the mutinous spirit and the ingratitude of the first Prince of the Blood. And so threatening were his demonstrations against the Flemish Government that Condé found it expedient to retire to Milan, leaving his wife under the guardianship of the true-hearted Isabella. When her husband had departed, Charlotte, at the instigation of the French agents—who were allowed free access to her—signed a petition to the Pope for the dissolution of her marriage. It must be said in her favour that the Prince's disposition and appearance were eminently fitted to repel the affection of flattered young beauty; and that she was led to believe that, should her suit prove successful, Henry would repudiate Mary of Medicis and make her Queen. But the murder of the French monarch by Ravaillac, on the 14th of May, 1610, in one of the narrow streets of Paris, dispelled her ambitious day-dreams. This tragic event—one of the strangest fulfilments known of the predictions of astrologers—secured the peace

of Europe for another decade. Though he had
not issued any declaration of war, Henry, when
he fell, was on the eve of setting out to execute
the ambitious and somewhat quixotic designs he
had laboriously and, as he thought, secretly matured
for the destruction of the house of Austria. He had
concluded alliances for the partition of the expected
spoils with Savoy, Venice, and the Protestant
States of Northern Germany. Two large and
well-appointed French armies only waited the
word of command to march into Germany and
Italy; and the enormous treasure amassed by
Sully's oppressive measures of finance was sufficient to support an obstinate struggle. Patriotic
French writers have lamented this monarch's untimely fate as a national calamity, in having
delayed the ascendency which, fifty years later,
their nation acquired in Europe. But it was most
fortunate for France that her part in a great
European conflict was deferred for twenty years.
The Spanish infantry was still invincible. Neither
Henry nor any of his generals was at all capable
of coping with Spinola; nor was there, as yet, a
Gustavus Adolphus in the North to scatter the
disciplined armies of the Emperor. The foundation of French supremacy required a more
favourable conjuncture of circumstances, and, the

agency of splendid and daring genius; the political genius of Cardinal Richelieu, and the military genius of the Great Condé.

After the death of Henry IV., Condé returned to France, and played a prominent part in the troubles that agitated the Regency of Mary of Medicis. He was a prince of considerable ability, and of a sagacity almost unerring to discern, amidst the turmoil of faction, the course most conducive to his own interests. Inheriting a very scanty patrimony, the great purpose of his life, of his habitual adulation of a strong government, and his habitual caballing against one which was weak, was the accumulation of wealth and dignities. And so skilfully did he steer his fortunes amidst the political shoals and quicksands of the perilous times in which he lived, so sedulously did he shift his sails for every favourable breeze, and so well was a grasping ambition seconded by economy which bordered on parsimony, that, long before his death, he held conjointly many of the greatest posts in the kingdom, and had amassed a colossal fortune.

His prudence, however, was not always able to ward off the reverses which chequer even the most successful careers. In 1616 he was arrested at the Louvre, by order of Mary of Medicis, and flung into the Bastille; from which fortress he was afterwards transferred to the Castle of Vincennes. Up to this time, the feud with his wife had been festering; her suit for a divorce was still pending in the Ecclesiastical Courts. But the Princess no sooner learned that misfortune had overwhelmed her husband than she hastened to his side. Compassion awakened in her breast the true instincts of a wife, and taught her to cherish ties she had striven with such impatience to rend asunder. The Regent would only permit her access to the Prince on condition that she remained to share his captivity. She consented to this sacrifice without a murmur, and, burying her youth and beauty for three years to brighten the gloom of his prison, won as much of his regard as it was possible for a woman to win.

Of several children, who were the fruit of this reconciliation, the eldest surviving son, Louis of Bourbon, Duke of Enghien, was born on the 7th September, 1621. His constitution was originally exceedingly feeble; but judicious nurture in the pure air of the Castle of Montrond' in Berri strengthened it to such a degree, that in after life he was capable of bearing the most extraordinary fatigues. From his early childhood there were discerned in him flashes of the quick genius and the haughty temper that characterised his manhood. In the Jesuit College at Bourges, where he was educated, he is said to have excelled all his companions in scholastic and scientific attainments, as well as in manly accomplishments. The house which he inhabited in the town, built by Jacques Cœur, the famous financier of the reign of Charles VII., was a magnificent relic of feudal architecture, and bore on its front in letters of stone the motto of the minister, " *A cœur vaillant rien impossible.*" No doubt this noble sentiment fed the aspiring fancies of the future hero. In the year 1639, when yet but eighteen years old, Enghien was summoned to take part in public affairs. The "Thirty Years' War" was raging in Germany. France, under the guidance of Cardinal Richelieu, had allied herself with Sweden against the Emperor and, later on, with Holland against Spain. The Prince of Condé, whose craving for military distinction far exceeded his military capacity, having obtained the command of the French army of Roussillon, delegated the government of Burgundy to his son. In the following year, the young Duke made his first campaign under Marshal La Meillerai, in Flanders, with great distinction. On returning to Paris, he went to Ruel to visit Cardinal Richelieu.

This great minister was now at the summit of power and glory. He had apparently trodden out the last embers of opposition in France. All classes, from the King to the peasant, bowed to his resistless will. His colossal schemes of policy had already been crowned with splendid success. At home, he had crushed with an iron hand the military republic which the Huguenots had established in the heart of the kingdom, and shattered the feudal dominion of the great nobles. Abroad, the fortunate star of the house of Austria had grown pale in the blaze of his genius. He had heard much of Enghien's ability. To test it, he engaged him for several hours in a discussion on the most difficult questions—religion, war, politics, government; and his reported comment on the conversation is so flattering to his visitor, that the very warmth of the panegyric suggests doubts as to its authenticity. He is said to have remarked to his favourite Chavigny, that Enghien would be the greatest man of his time, perhaps of any time, in all things. It is certain, however, that the young prince made a most favourable impression on him. It was a great object of his ambition to ally his family with the royal blood of France. The Prince of Condé, with the keen instinct of self-aggrandisement peculiar to himself, divined this wish, and humbly besought the all-powerful minister to consent to a marriage between his niece Claire de Maillé Brezé and Enghien. Claire, who was but thirteen years old, and child-like for her age, inspired Enghien with a feeling of contemptuous aversion. But the reluctant bridegroom did not dare to offer remonstrance, and, notwithstanding the tender years of the young lady, the marriage was celebrated in the King's chapel in February, 1641.

The year following Enghien accompanied Louis 13th in the successful campaign which added Roussillon to the French crown. When the armies had retired into winter quarters, he became, it is said, the chief actor in a ludicrous interlude, which furnishes an amusing illustration of the remarkable ascendency of Richelieu.

In passing through Lyons, on his return to the capital, he had neglected to pay his respects to the Cardinal Archbishop of the city, who was the brother of the Prime Minister. The latter, when Enghien next went to visit him at Ruel, inquired after his relative; and the Duke was obliged to confess his sin of omission. Richelieu made no remark at the moment, but afterwards mentioned the slight in angry terms to the Prince of Condé. The Prince, terrified to the last degree, ordered his son instantly to repair the neglect; and Enghien, in obedience to the paternal injunction, started off without delay to Lyons—a journey of two hundred leagues, over execrable roads, rendered almost impassable by the rains of autumn. The Archbishop, having been seasonably forewarned of this pilgrimage, seized, perhaps, with more than usual compassion for his hungry flock, or anxious to escape so much honour, considerately set out for Marseilles. Here, at the utmost verge of the arch-diocese, he received his distinguished visitor with a truly edifying humility. When Enghien had returned to Paris from his penitential mission, Richelieu, labouring under a second access of fraternal solicitude, renewed his inquiries; but on learning from such an excellent authority as the son of the First Prince of the Blood that the Archbishop was in perfect health, he appears to have recovered his wonted composure.

At the end of the same year the great Cardinal died, worn out by the attacks of an excruciating malady. On his death-bed he recommended Cardinal Mazarin to Louis XIII. as his successor; and Mazarin, in order to secure his unstable position by the powerful support of the House of Condé, obtained for its young heir the command of the army which was opposed to the Spaniards on the Flemish frontier. Enghien, having thus attained the great object of his young ambition, set out early in the year 1643 for the scene of action, a field on which he was to reap immortal glory.

The empire which the Spaniards reared during the 15th and 16th centuries, was, perhaps, the most splendid and far-spreading that the world has ever seen. It comprised the most beautiful, flourishing, and civilized regions of Europe. It spread over rich and extensive islands, breathing the fragrance and bright with the glowing vegetation of a tropical clime ; some of which, until the close of the 15th century, had slept in virgin beauty, still fresh from the hand of Nature, in the embrace of an unknown ocean. And beyond this ocean it extended over boundless realms of a new world, the wealth and magnificence of which were hardly exaggerated by popular fancy that pictured them paved with gems, flowing with rivers of gold, realising the enchanted dreams of Eastern poets. Every sea of which the enterprise of Europe had made a pathway was subject to Spanish sway. It was the Castilian who first uttered the proud boast that on the dominions of his sovereign the sun never set. Profound statesmanship and consummate military skill were the architects of this splendid fabric ; as they had built up other vast empires long crumbled into dust. In truth, not even Rome, in her palmiest days, produced, within an equal period, a larger number of great public men than the Spanish Monarchy could show during the glorious reigns of Ferdinand

and Isabella the Catholic, Charles I., and Philip
II. Standing out in brighter radiance from the
illustrious throng, are the undying forms of
the Emperor-King, Gonsalvo of Cordova, Chris-
topher Columbus and Hernan Cortes, Cardinals
Zimenes and Granvelle, Alva and Pescara, Don
John of Austria, the type of Christian heroism,
Alexander Farnese, the type of the finished
warrior and statesman. And Spain can point with
pride to what Rome never possessed, a splendid
original literature and a splendid school of art.

But, in addition to the genius for command, and
the practical energy which are common in a greater
or less degree to all conquering races, there was
in the Spanish Monarchy a peculiar and vital
element, which constituted at once its strength
and its idiosyncrasy. This was the spirit of
enthusiasm, religious and romantic, which had
informed its growth, and which vivified its matu-
rity. For more than eight centuries the peninsula
had been the battle-ground of the Crescent and
the Cross, the theatre of a long crusade. In the
7th century the Arabs crossing over from Africa,
overturned the kingdom of the Goths, and
established on its ruins the magnificent Empire of
the Western Caliphs. Christianity and Gothic
freedom, driven from the plains, retired into the
Northern Sierras, and throned in these "eternal

palaces of nature," breathed indomitable valour into generations of heroes, who descended year after year to maintain a desperate struggle for their country and their God. From the day on which the standard of Don Roderick was cloven down on the banks of the Guadelete, to that on which the standard of Ferdinand and Isabella floated by the side of the Cross from the walls of the Alhambra, the Holy War raged with little interruption. During this long period the sublime frenzy, born of burning faith and restless daring, which, seizing at intervals, like an intermittent fever, on colder nations of Europe, had whitened the plains of Asia Minor, and the Syrian and African deserts, with the bones of myriads of warrior-pilgrims, was in the Spaniard but the natural pulsation of life. His whole career was a combat for glory and the Cross. In him the spirit of chivalry found its grandest and purest embodiment. He lived in an ideal world—in the charmed land of Romance. Even the common incidents of war, touched by the magic hues of his fancy, were invested with an unreal aspect; while his bold, imaginative temperament, kindled by peril and exalted by faith, indued him with power to accomplish, in his long struggle with the Moors, feats which read on the sober page of history like the myths of heroic fable. And after

Grenada had fallen before the arms of Ferdinand and Isabella, this adventurous spirit and this fervid zeal sought out and found a wider field of action. Little bands of warriors, bearing the banner of the Cross, launched out upon the bosom of a trackless ocean, and discovered and conquered for Catholicity and Spain realms richer and more vast than had mocked the dreams of Alexander. It was soon apparent, too, in European warfare, that no other troops could withstand the shock of battalions, in which the fierce enthusiasm of the crusader, curbed by a perfect discipline, had mellowed into the calm feeling of invincibility inspired by a hundred victories. Wherever the Spaniards fought they conquered; and in fifty years after the downfall of Grenada they had won the most splendid empire that the world had seen since the Goth had scaled the Alps, and the Hun had stalled his war steed in the palaces of Cæsar.

The great empires of the earth have each had a peculiar mission: each has been an instrument fashioned by a Divine hand for the achievement of some special design, accomplished by the force of its own natural development. The events of the 16th century called into play, in all their vigour, the characteristic genius and the matured energies of the Spanish monarchy.

The 16th century was for the Catholic church

a period of marvellous peril, and still more marvellous triumph. Century after century had the storms of the world raged in wild fury around the chair of Peter; but never since the terrible times when the Christian slave slunk tremblingly at night from out of the marble palaces of Imperial Rome, to worship amidst the bones of martyrs in the gloom of the Catacombs, had its deep foundations been assailed by so rude a tempest. At once, from every point of the horizon, the wide ruin burst upon it. North, South, East, and West, hereditary foes, or revolted subjects, the Christian and the Infidel, conspired its overthrow. In Germany, the Reformation, arising like a wintry torrent which leaps forth from a scanty spring and gathers volume as it rushes on rolled its turbid tide over the greater part of civilized Europe, until its baffled waves surged against the impassable barriers of the Alps and the Pyrenees. In the East, Solyman the Magnificent, the greatest of the able and warlike line that filled the throne of Mahomet II., conquered Hungary, captured Rhodes, and avowed the design of planting the standard of the Prophet on the Palatine. From the South, Barbary Corsairs ravaged with impunity the beautiful shores of Campania, and swept shrieking peasants into captivity from beneath the walls of Rome. At one time it seemed well-nigh certain, humanly speaking, that victorious Protestantism must trample the Papacy under foot. For a considerable period, it was probable that the lapse of a single year might see the Crescent glittering above the ruins of St. Peter's. But to the Catholic the event of this mortal conflict only furnished another proof of the weakness of human power, and the folly of human policy, when directed against a supernatural institution, built and sustained by Divine hands. It confirmed his belief that there is in the bosom of Catholicity a spring of immortal life which neither external force nor internal corruption can destroy. The sacrilegious hand that would break up the fountain causes it to flow in purer and more abundant channels. Gaudy weeds, nourished by the foul breath of the world, may, indeed, for a time, mantle and choke it with their rank luxuriance; but the keen blast of adversity shrivels them up, and the living waters leap forth again, bright and joyous, an eternal source of youth and vigour. The Church, quivering in every member, but aroused from a fatal lethargy by the shock of so many enemies, armed herself with her keenest weapons. The efforts of her faithful children first stemmed, then rolled back the tide of destruction that had threatened to overwhelm her. And in this terrible struggle her foremost champions in spiritual warfare, as on the field of battle, were Spaniards; the great Spanish monarchy was her right arm and her shield. At the danger of the Church the old crusading spirit which had so often kindled the Spaniard's blood into fire leaped with electric power through every rank, from the peasant to the King. Spain drove back Protestantism in France and the Netherlands, and gave the mightiest impulse to the great Catholic reaction, which advanced with victorious banner to the borders of Scandinavia. From her ports went forth the illustrious Captain and the bulk of the great Armada that shattered the Ottoman power at Lepanto. And it was a Spaniard, at once the truest representative of the religious spirit of his race, with its lofty enthusiasm, its disciplined strength, and its indomitable energy, and the grandest religious figure of modern times, who founded the order of Jesus, the history of which is the history of the triumphs and the reverses of the Catholic Church in every region of either hemisphere.

Between this great monarchy, from its earliest consolidation, and the neighbouring kingdom of France, there had existed an intense national rivalry. At first the conflict was not unequal. The struggles of the two nations for superiority deluged a large part of civilized Europe with blood, and especially desolated the classic land of Italy, where genius, drinking at perennial fountains of inspiration, has in every age crowned the indestructible beauty of nature with imperishable garlands. But, after a time, the preponderance of Spain became unquestionable. Her vast resources, the profound policy of her rulers, the consummate ability of her generals, the disciplined valour of her troops, filled the rest of Europe with a well-founded fear that she would achieve universal dominion. In the obstinate and oftenrenewed warfare the power of France was crippled by memorable reverses at Pavia and St. Quentin. The Huguenot convulsion which followed the death of Henry II. prostrated her at the feet of her hereditary foe. But after the death of Philip II. of Spain his throne was occupied by a degenerate line, and the influence of a pure despotism, administered by weak and corrupt hands, was apparent in the rapid decay of his empire. The liberties of Castile cloven down under the regency of Cardinal Zimines at the battle of Villalar, the liberties of Arragon crushed by Philip II., had never been permitted to bud forth again. The old crusading spirit was now out of date. The monarchy had accomplished its peculiar mission ; the great Catholic reaction had spent its force. There no longer existed within the state either a strong vital principle or a regenerating element. With the hardy love of adventure, born of popular freedom and elevated by religious zeal, the lust of conquest had also passed away. The riches of Mexico and Peru enervated the iron energies which a world in arms could not subdue. And when the mighty genius of Richelieu, having stifled anarchy at home, directed the united strength of France to humble her old rival, it was seen how languid was the life-current that animated a colossal frame; how rapidly the powerful empire of Philip II. was collapsing into a nerveless mass, terrible only in the prestige of former glories. Still, however, the superb monarchy preserved its vast proportions. Internal revolution or foreign aggression had, as yet, scarcely torn a gem from the haughty diadem of Spain and the Indies. The fairest regions of Europe, the realms subdued by Cortez and Pizarro, where the soil teemed with precious stones and the rivers flowed over sands of gold, remained subject to its sway. Castilian pride and prowess still awakened emotions of hatred and fear in every known region of the globe.

The Spanish army which Enghien was charged to oppose consisted of twenty-seven thousand veteran troops under the command of Don Francisco de Melo, an experienced general. De Melo had laid siege to Rocroi, a frontier town of considerable strength, embosomed in the forest of Ardennes. It was the key of the province of Champagne, and its capture would open the road to Paris. The young duke marched with twenty-two thousand men to relieve the place; and neither the news of the death of Louis XIII., which reached him on his way, with positive orders from the Government not to risk a battle, nor the cautious counsels of the old Marshal l'Hopital, who had been appointed to restrain his well-known impetuosity, checked the rapidity of his movements. He was determined to fight at all hazards.

The Spaniards had pitched their camp on an uneven plain of small extent, surrounded on all sides by woods and marshes, and crowned by the beleaguered fortress. Their position, which could only be approached through a narrow defile, was naturally almost impregnable. But De Melo was himself too anxious for battle to avail himself of his advantages of ground for the purpose of defence. Confiding in the superior numbers and the tried valour of his troops, and well informed of the critical state of affairs in Paris, he had resolved to terminate the war by a decisive blow. He therefore permitted the French army to pour without molestation through the narrow pass, and encamp on a small eminence fronting his own position. Evening was closing in, and both sides prepared for a decisive battle at break of day.

Marshal l'Hopital, terrified at Enghien's rashness in exposing his troops to the assault of a superior enemy in a position in which defeat was destruction, earnestly besought him to draw back while there was yet time. But the duke, surrounded by young French nobles as eager for glory as himself, and having the support of General Gassion, the most able and enterprising of his lieutenants, peremptorily over-ruled his mentor's opposition. He had determined to return to Paris a conqueror or a corpse. On the other side, De Melo unwisely refused to await the arrival of General Beck, who, with a detached wing of his army, was hastening back to his aid.

The night was cold and dim, but soon the whole plain blazed with watch-fires, which flung a ruddy blush on the lowering heavens, the sombre foliage and the white walls of the besieged town. As the night rolled on, the scene was one that, even in the mind of a war-worn veteran, might well have awakened feelings of solemn awe. The majestic woods ranged around in a sylvan amphitheatre, here frowning in dense masses, here standing out gaunt and spectral in the flickering light, looked down mournfully on that tranquil plain, so soon to be rent by the fury and strewn with the wrecks of war, to become the grave of a great empire; but where now the death-like stillness resting on the armed hosts, and sadly suggestive of the deeper and more appalling silence that would close the strife of the morrow, was rendered palpable rather than broken by the mighty respiration of profound slumber, floating in a drowsy hum upon the air, or the occasional boom of a cannon from the distant ramparts, echoing in dying thunder through the leafy aisles of the forest. And in addition to the sobering influence which the mournful magic of that scene and hour would naturally fling over the unseared mind of a general of two and twenty on the eve of his first battle, there were special anxieties incidental to Enghien's situation sufficient to disturb the composure of the most veteran captain. He was about, with inferior forces, and, contrary to the advice of his oldest officers, to fight a battle on which the safety not only of his army but of his country depended. Opposed to him were generals grown grey in war, on ground selected by themselves; and above all he had to confront the renowned Spanish infantry, those famous tercios who, since the days of the Great Captain, had been the terror and admiration of the world. On their serried ranks the stormiest wave of battle had hitherto broken in vain. No foeman had ever seen their backs. They had driven the Arabs from the mosques of Cordova; they had shivered the idols in the temples of the Incas; they had crushed the great Lutheran League at Muhlberg; they had tamed the pride of Islam on the banks of the Danube. Often before had the flower of French chivalry recoiled from their iron columns like raging surf from a rugged cliff. Whenever hitherto the battle had wavered, the shock of the tercios, united as one man, had turned the tide. For a century and a half they had been invincible, and in truth it needed extraordinary genius or extraordinary incapacity to outweigh so much disciplined valour.

But the mind of the young hero, naturally somewhat hard and selfish, was as undisturbed as if it had found in peril its proper element. Flinging himself on the ground by a watch-fire, he was soon buried in such profound slumber that his attendants aroused him with difficulty at break of day. Before the dawn of the 20th of May, 1643, both armies were drawn out in battle array. The formation of both was that usual at the time; the strength of the cavalry was disposed on the wings, the strength of the infantry in the centre.

On the right wing of the French, Enghien commanded in person, with Gassion as second in command. In place of a helmet he wore a hat adorned with large white plumes. Marshal l'Hopital led the French left, Baron d'Espenan the centre, and Baron de Sirot the reserves. This last general was a Burgundian, famous throughout the army for his boast that in each of three pitched battles he had encountered a king, and had borne away as trophies of his personal prowess the hat of Gustavus Adolphus, the scarf of the King of Poland, and the pistol of the King of Denmark.

The right of the Spanish army, composed mainly of German horse, was led by Don Francisco de Melo. The Duke of Albuquerque, a distinguished officer, was stationed on the left with the Walloon Cavalry. The tercios were in the centre; their renowned leader, the Count of Fuentes, oppressed by age and infirmities, reclined on a litter in the midst of his veteran bands. De Melo, taking advantage of the hollow and wooded ground that separated the hostile camps, placed a thousand musketeers in ambush, with orders to fall on Enghien's flank and rear in the heat of the fight.

The trumpets having sounded, the battle began simultaneously on both wings. Enghien, having penetrated the tactics of his adversary, made a detour to the right, cut in pieces the musketeers

who lay sheltered in a copse-wood, and then
dashing forward with the rapidity of a whirlwind,
charged the Spanish left in front and flank.
Albuquerque's Walloons were borne down by the
impetuosity of the attack, and scattered over the
plain like withered leaves drifting in the blasts of
autumn. On the other wing, De Melo, with equal
vigour and success, drove l'Hopital's squadrons
from the field; routed Espenan's infantry; captured all the French artillery; and then fell with
fury on the reserves. The situation appeared so
desperate that several of his officers urged Baron
Sirot to fly, assuring him that the day was lost.
"No," replied the Burgundian, "the day is not
lost, for Sirot and his comrades have yet to fight."
But notwithstanding the most heroic efforts, the
French reserves, pressed on all sides, began to
waver, and disastrous rout seemed inevitable along
the whole line.

Tidings of the critical state of the battle were
brought to Enghien, while he was still in hot pursuit of Albuquerque's cavalry. It was a moment
to test decisively the capacity of a leader. But
Enghien, like Julius Cæsar, was born a great
general. One flash of inspiration showed him the
road to victory, one mighty impulse of impetuous
valour carried him to the goal. Gathering together his squadrons, he led them at full gallop

behind the Spanish centre, and hurled them like a thunderbolt against De Melo's rear. The shock and the surprise of an assault from warriors who appeared to have started out of the earth, were irresistible. Rider and horse went down in the crash of this terrible onset. The French cavalry cleft like an iron wedge through the midst of the enemy; then, wheeling right and left, rode them down in masses. The plain was strewed with the broken ranks. De Melo's whole wing was shattered to pieces, and the General, casting away his baton of command, saved himself with difficulty by the speed of his horse.

But the battle was not yet over. It still remained to vanquish the Spanish infantry which, drawn up in a solid square, had hitherto stood motionless, haughty and menacing, but calm in the heroic pride of a hundred triumphs, a dark cloud charged with the lightning of war. Enghien surveyed these stern warriors for some time with admiration mingled with anxiety; but while he hesitated to attack them, information reached him of the approach of General Beck's division. It was clear that he had no more time to lose. Having first ordered a furious cannonade with all his guns, to break in pieces the serried lines of the enemy, he collected his cavalry into one mass and threw it on the Spanish square. The Spaniards remained motionless till their assailants had come to within fifty feet; then their ranks opening, vomited forth a hissing torrent of flame and death that swept away the French by entire squadrons. So terrible was the carnage and confusion in the French ranks, that a charge of the German or Walloon horse must have totally changed the fortunes of the day. But these were already far away from the field, and Enghien rallied his men with extraordinary promptitude. Again and yet again the French artillery thundered, and in the pauses of the cannonade, the French cavalry charged with the most brilliant courage into the gaps which the shot had torn, roused to the highest pitch of enthusiasm by the example of their young leader, who rode in the foremost line, his white plumes floating above the thickest of the fight, a foam-streak cresting the red wave of battle. Again and a third time the choicest troops of France were scattered in frightful disarray, or fell in heaps, mowed down by the iron tempest that burst from that fatal square. It was then that the Count of Fuentes showed with what grandeur a noble spirit can rise superior to the infirmities of the body, and the pangs of death itself. Broken by years and sickness, and covered with wounds, the old General continued, with serene fortitude, to issue his orders from the litter that was soaked with his blood, and to sustain his old companions in arms by voice and example. The brave tercios, girdled by their rampart of fire, sternly closed up their thinning ranks after each furious onset, and again awaited, with unfaltering resolution, the shock of the foe.

At last Enghien bringing up all his forces, horse, foot, and artillery, assailed the Spaniards on every side. But the Spanish officers now saw that further resistance could only result in useless slaughter. Their best men had fallen; Fuentes was expiring of his wounds; and there was no longer a hope of succour. The fugitive cavalry, meeting in its flight the advancing troops of General Beck, had communicated to them its own panic, and hurried them along in such headlong rout, that all the cannon and baggage of the division was abandoned to an unseen enemy. The Spanish officers, therefore, expressed by signs a wish to surrender. Enghien, overjoyed, advanced alone to accept their submission. But the Spanish soldiers, mistaking his friendly gestures for hostile signals, received him with a terrible volley of musketry. He escaped by a miracle. The French, enraged at this seeming perfidy, rushed forward to avenge it, and numbers fell before the exertions of the officers on both sides could stay the slaughter. The surviving Spaniards surrendered.

Such was the victory of Rocroi, one of the most glorious and decisive in history. It was the death-blow of the great Spanish monarchy. The renowned tercios, so long its prop and pride, were here annihilated. A Spanish officer, on being asked after the battle what had been their strength in the morning, answered with a mournful pride, "You have only to count the dead and the prisoners." Spain henceforth was unable to maintain the leading position which for more than a century she had held. From the battle of Rocroi dates that decided military superiority of the French which has more than once menaced the independence of Europe.

CHAPTER II.

AFTER this great victory, Enghien proposed to over-run Flanders, which lay open to invasion. But the boldness of the project was distasteful to the Council of State, then distracted by the dissensions that preceded the elevation of Cardinal Mazarin to the supreme conduct of affairs; and he was compelled to restrict his operations to the seige of Thionville, one of the strongest fortresses in Europe, which commanded the course of the Moselle to the gates of Treves. The fall of this important town, after a stubborn defence, terminated the campaign. Anne of Austria, overjoyed at splendid successes which had established her Regency with so much *éclat*, heaped favours on the young conqueror. She gave him the government of Champagne and the town of Stenay; and at his request, Gassion, his able though somewhat impracticable lieutenant, received a Marshal's baton.

The extraordinary career of Gassion, one of the greatest soldiers France has produced, deserves a brief notice. Alone of the celebrated generals who created the military power of Louis XIV., he owed nothing of his success to birth or family interest. Valour and capacity raised him when still young, in spite of unusual personal and political disadvantages, from the grade of a private soldier to that of Marshal of France. He was the son of a President of the Parliament of Pau. His father destined him for the legal profession, but at the age of fifteen he ran away from home and enlisted. His bravery and good conduct soon won commendation; but the rude independence of his character, and his strong attachment to the Huguenot faith, coupled with his plebeian origin, opposed an almost insuperable bar to his advancement. Fortunately for him he attracted the notice of Cardinal Richelieu, whose eye was ever quick to discern merit, and who was indulgent to heretical opinions when they did not menace the welfare of the State. The Cardinal, admiring the military talents and the rough frankness of the young Gascon, gave him his confidence and esteem, pushed him on to high commands, and was fond of comparing him to his celebrated countryman, Bertrand de Guesclin. He used to add that Gassion was free from the coarseness that sullied the splendid qualities of Charles V.'s famous Constable. Though Gassion obtained his Marshal's baton upon the recommendation of Enghien, his insubordination afterwards provoked a quarrel with his imperious commander. Incapable of flattery or even of discretion, he gave mortal offence to Cardinal Mazarin by publicly deriding the all-powerful minister's pretentions to military knowledge; and there is but little doubt that long before his death he would have fallen into complete disgrace, had his genius been less remarkable, or less necessary to the State. He was killed in 1647, while besieging the small town of Lens, and, as has been well remarked by a native historian, " France in gaining a hamlet lost a hero."

During Enghien's absence at the siege of Thionville, his young wife was delivered of a son. He, who only the previous year might have been seen playing at children's games in the saloons of the capital, returned to them with the most glorious name in Europe, and found all Paris at his feet.

There has never existed in any other country of Europe a condition of society approaching in intellectual brilliancy and extravagant debauchery, that of the French capital during the Regency of Anne of Austria. Never before or since has there been seen collected together such versatile genius, such sparkling wit, such spiritual beauty adorned with every charm except virtue, such coarse frivolity, such reckless ferocity, such universal and shameless laxity of principle. The melancholy and austere character of Louis XIII.; his long estrangement from his wife, which banished gaiety and pomp from the silent halls of the Louvre, and the iron rule of his Minister had exercised a stifling influence on French society. Richelieu himself was a most munificent friend of literature and the fine arts, and delighted in brilliant festivals and pageants. He loved to assemble all who were distinguished or attractive in the magnificent halls of the Palais Cardinal, or at Ruel, where every form of costly and refined enjoyment charmed the fancy and gratified the most fastidious taste. But ever engrossed with the cares of government and the active direction of military operations, his occasional example was insufficient to counteract the effects of a state of continual foreign and domestic strife, a harsh and cheerless court, and a sternly repressive rule. The young, beautiful, and accomplished Marchioness of Rambouillet had indeed already formed the celebrated circle which for purity of tone, combined with the highest charms of cultivated intellect, and feminine grace, has never been rivalled. In the saloons of the Hotel Rambouillet might be seen, amidst a dazzling crowd of minor luminaries,

Voiture; Corneille, now at the summit of his fame; Moliere, La Fontaine, Boileau, who had already achieved their first laurels; Bossuet rising into celebrity, and, later on, Pascal. But the standard of thought and refinement in this circle was too high for any but the choicer spirits of the time, and its influence did not touch the general mass of the high-born and wealthy.

At the commencement of the Regency, however, Parisian society, relieved from the frigid asceticism of Louis XIII., and the iron pressure of Richelieu, burst forth with a wayward vigour and a wild licentiousness, which went on increasing in force and extravagance till they culminated in the frantic excesses of the Fronde. The Court presented an appearance of festivity and splendour unknown since the palmy days of Catherine of Medicis. Brilliant, beautiful, and dissolute women, the Duchess of Chevreuse, the Duchess of Montbazon, the Princess Palatine, and others belonging to the highest rank of nobility, who had been forced into exile or obscurity in the previous reign, reappeared in Paris, and threw open their saloons, in which the strife of love, of politics, of vanity, of cupidity, raged without restraint. It was an age of extraordinary characters. The most celebrated personages of either sex who illustrated the times of Louis XIV. grew up, or were matured, amidst the bold license in which the social and political life of France rioted during the regency of his mother. The young hero of Rocroi found himself, on his return to the capital, the central figure of intoxicating scenes, which flattered his self-esteem and stimulated his passions. Loaded with honours and caresses by the Regent and Cardinal Mazarin, idolized by his own family, courted and followed on every side by those who were themselves objects of adulation, disliking and despising his wife, he plunged into the dissipations which spread their allurements before him, with all the ardour of his fiery nature. The queens of beauty and fashion welcomed the young hero with their brightest smiles; and there gathered around him, as their natural chief, a brilliant band of debauched young nobles, many of whom afterwards became famous. De Grammont, Bussy, Rabutin, Marsillac, better known as La Rochefoucault, Chatillon, and his brother Coligny. Boutteville, renowned in later years as Duke of Luxembourg, Turenne, were constantly seen in his train. His person and bearing were well adapted to sustain the admiration excited by his great achievements. He was above the middle stature, was perfectly well-made, and excelled in all graceful and manly exercises. He had a magnificent head. Large blue eyes, bright and piercing as those of an eagle, and an aquiline nose lent to his countenance a singular character of command. His mouth, which was too large, and expressed the harshness and want of sensibility which disfigured his disposition, detracted from the haughty beauty of his face; but the vivacity of his glance and the sparkling gaiety of his conversation, soon caused its disagreeable effect to be forgotten. There was something great and lofty in his whole appearance and demeanour, which discovered, even to a stranger, a proud and indomitable soul.

The family of Condé consisted of the old Prince and Princess; Enghien with his wife and son; a daughter, Anne Genevieve of Bourbon, two years older than the Duke; and a second son, his junior by eight years.

Mademoiselle de Bourbon, one of the loveliest women of the age, was married to the Duke of Longueville, a nobleman old enough to be her father, but of great hereditary possessions and influence, who represented an illegitimate branch of the royal line, and one of the most worthy of the national heroes, the famous Count Dunois. Her beauty consisted not so much in perfection of feature, as in that combination of colouring and expression, of tender grace and soft brilliancy, which is most potent over the hearts of men. It was impossible, according to the confession of a lady who was her contemporary and not her friend, to see her without loving and wishing to please her. The mild radiance of her blue eyes, rich and lustrous as a turquoise, the dazzling bloom of a complexion in which the lily and the rose were exquisitely blended; the masses of golden hair that crowned her loveliness, as with a glory, the delicate symmetry of her form, and an undulating grace which made its movements the poetry of motion, ravished the eyes of the beholder, like an angelic vision. Her personal attractions were enhanced by wit, talent, and considerable accomplishments. Her brothers were attached to her with passionate devotion, and the most distinguished young nobles of the Court ardently contended for her favour. But her conduct had been above reproach, until a tragical incident which occurred at this time changed the whole tenour of her life.

During the summer of 1643 the struggle for power between Anne of Austria's old allies, the party of the ancient noblesse, under the leadership of Madame de Chevreuse and the young Duke of Beaufort, grandson of Henry IV., and the party of Cardinal Richelieu, of which the Prince of Condé and Cardinal Mazarin were chiefs, convulsed the Court and city. The Princess of

Condé and Richelieu's accomplished niece, the Duchess of Aiguillon, gave efficient support to the cause to which family interest linked them; but the vast majority of the great ladies of the capital were vehement partizans of the feudal party, popularly known as the "Importants." Conspicuous amongst these ladies for bold and dazzling beauty, and for resolute audacity which scorned the restraints of prudence, was the young Duchess of Montbazon, wife of the aged Governor of Paris, who was father of Madame de Chevreuse, by an earlier marriage. Magnificent dark hair and eyes, a brilliant complexion heightened by art, and a majestic figure, commanded for Madame de Montbazon the admiration and homage of the whole Court. Beaufort was a passionate and favoured lover of hers; and even the Duke of Longueville wore her chains. The fresher charms, the more exalted rank, the spotless fame of Madame de Longueville, her reputation in the fastidious circle of the Hotel Rambouillet, and her quiet contempt for attractions which borrowed so largely from art, excited Madame de Montbazon's jealousy and anger. Not content with enticing to her feet the husband of her rival, she resolved to blast her name. One evening two letters were picked up in the crowded saloons of the Hotel de Montbazon, and carried to the hostess.

No one approaching to claim them, the Duchess glanced over their contents, and proposed to read them aloud for the amusement of her guests. They were anonymous epistles from a lady to her lover, reproaching him for his coldness, and his ingratitude for past favours. The Duchess having finished the reading, amidst laughter, coarse jests, and satirical conjectures regarding the writer, declared that the letters were in the handwriting of Madame de Longueville, and that they had been dropped by Count Coligny, who had just quitted the apartment. This statement, though a mere calumny, as was made manifest shortly afterwards by the voluntary confession of one of the real lovers, was quickly circulated in whispered confidences by frail sisters, and with rude jibes and merriment by the Duke of Beaufort and his boisterous companions. In the heated state of the political atmosphere, the springing of a mine beneath the city could not have filled it with greater tumult and dismay than did the broaching of this slander. The House of Condé and its powerful connexion prepared to right the injured lady, if necessary, by the force of arms. Enghien, then before Thionville, despatched a challenge to Beaufort, and, without waiting for the Regent's permission, set out for Paris to avenge his sister. The allies of the

Houses of Vendome, Guise and Montbazon, in short the whole party of the Importants, rallied around the vindictive Duchess. The capital would have been deluged with blood had not the Regent promptly intervened and treated the quarrel as an affair of State. She sent a messenger to stop Enghien, with the assurance that she assumed to herself the duty of vindicating the honour of a Bourbon princess; and then commanded Madame de Montbazon to deliver up the letters to her, and to make a public apology to the Princess of Condé. The Duchess was forced to submit. The letters were read aloud at Court by Cardinal Mazarin, and then committed by Anne of Austria to the flames. Madame de Chevreuse, on behalf of her step-daughter, and Mazarin on the part of the Queen, met in a room of the Louvre, and, after a wrangling discussion of many hours, agreed on the terms in which reparation was to be made. On the appointed day Madame de Montbazon, attended by Beaufort and a splendid train of cavaliers, repaired to the Hotel de Condé, where all the world of Paris was assembled. The written apology, which she was to read aloud, was pinned, as previously agreed, to the inside of her fan. The princess, the living type of calm dignity and aristocratic pride, and still adorned with much of the peerless beauty which had thrown half Europe into confusion, awaited her unwilling visitor in State at the furthest end of the crowded saloon, with Cardinal Mazarin at her side as representative of the Regent. The Duchess slowly advanced towards them with an air of insolent levity; pronounced the words in mocking tones; and then, surrounded by her brilliant escort, swept in superb disdain from the room. The deliberate insult of this proceeding aggravated the original offence; and the Princess obtained permission from the Queen to absent herself from every place of resort where she might be forced to endure the presence of her fair enemy. As Madame de Condé, by her rank, lofty character, political influence, and close intimacy with Anne of Austria, was in reality, though not in name, the second lady in France, this arrangement excluded the Duchess of Montbazon from society on all occasions of Court festivity or State ceremonial. Deeply mortified she determined to resist.

The most fashionable place of public resort at that time in Paris was a pleasure garden, called the "Jardin Renard," close to the Seine, at the bottom of the Tuileries Gardens. It was the custom of the high world to repair thither on summer evenings after the promenade on Cours la Reine, and solace themselves with feasting, music, and flirtations. The Duchess of Chevreuse

one evening invited the Queen and the Princess
of Condé to sup with her in this garden. As
they approached the pavilion reserved for them
Madame de Montbazon came forth from it to
receive them. The princess was about to retire,
but the Queen requested Madame de Chevreuse
to induce her step-daughter to withdraw. But
this self-willed lady flatly refused, and persisted
in accosting Anne of Austria, who waved her off
with an angry gesture, and quitted the Garden.
The Regent dearly loved dainty cheer; and her
wrath was not diminished on hearing how the
Duchess, after her departure, had seated herself,
in high spirits, and feasted on the delicacies provided for the royal party. On the following day
the rebellious beauty received an order of banishment from Paris, and her exile was speedily
followed by the ruin of her faction. When
Enghien returned to Court, Beaufort was a prisoner at Vincennes; but, at his instigation,
Count Coligni challenged the Duke of Guise,
who was accused, though apparently with injustice, of having been concerned in disseminating
the slander about Madame de Longueville. Notwithstanding the severe laws against duelling,
enacted by Cardinal Richelieu, the combatants
met at three o'clock in the afternoon in the centre
of the Place Royale, then the most fashionable

quarter of Paris. After a few passes, Coligni fell, mortally wounded. At a window over-looking the scene might be discerned a half-concealed form of exquisite grace, agitated by powerful emotion; a face of almost seraphic beauty clouded over by anxiety, and terror, and despair. It was Madame de Longueville watching the encounter, and the mortal agony of her champion, the ill-starred victim of the baffled vengeance of her family, and his own fatal passion. The unhappy notoriety which attached to her on account of these events had a most disastrous influence on Madame de Longueville's subsequent career.

With politics, Enghien meddled little during the lifetime of his father. It was a field for which his natural disposition did not fit him. He had neither the patience, nor the tact, nor the steadiness of purpose required for political success. Brought up in great awe of his father, who had grown grey in intrigue, he submissively bowed to the old Prince's experience in matters of State policy; and Condé lost none of his opportunities, as President of the Council of State and chief prop of Cardinal Mazarin, for advancing the interests of his house. The Princess' was the bosom friend of Anne of Austria. Wholly devoted to her glorious son, she strove to forward even his unreasonable aims and caprices with untiring ardour. War and pleasure—the perils and hardships of a bloody and brilliant campaign, followed by the soft and turbulent delights of Parisian society, chiefly filled up the four years of his life that followed his first memorable achievement in arms.

In the spring of 1644, France had armies on foot against the Spaniards, in Italy, on the Flemish frontier, and in Catalonia, which had revolted from the Spanish crown; and in Germany against the Emperor and the Elector of Bavaria. The army of Flanders would naturally have fallen to Enghien had not the Duke of Orleans, the King's uncle, and Lieutenant-General of the Kingdom, jealous of the renown of his young cousin, suddenly claimed the command. Enghien, therefore, to his intense mortification, found himself condemned to inaction at the head of a few thousand men on the borders of Luxembourg, until the disasters of the French arms in Germany called him to a sphere more worthy of his genius.

In November of the preceding year the Bavarians and Imperialists, under their famous generals, Count Mercy and John of Werth, had, though inferior in strength, fallen on the army of Marshal Rantzau, at Teutlingen, put it to complete rout, captured its commander and his chief officers while they were at dinner, and all its artillery and baggage. The French Court dispatched Viscount Turenne to repair this great misfortune. Turenne, the younger brother of the Duke of Bouillon, was ten years older than Enghien, and had greatly distinguished himself in Italy. Notwithstanding all his efforts, he was only able to collect, in the spring of 1644, about ten thousand of Rantzau's men, demoralised by defeat, wretchedly equipped, and in want of all necessary stores. Mercy, with fifteen thousand men, laid siege to Fribourg, in the Briesgau, and the French General, unable to offer any effectual opposition, appealed to Cardinal Mazarin for reinforcements. Thereupon Enghien was ordered to march into Germany with ten thousand fresh troops, and assume the chief command.

When the young Duke joined Turenne, he found that Fribourg had surrendered, and that Mercy had intrenched himself in an apparently impregnable position before the town. The campaigns that followed between Enghien and Mercy have especial interest, because never probably before or since have the merits of the French and German soldiers been so fairly tested. The armies, though small, were of the best quality, and not unequal in numbers. The Germans were all veterans, trained in the Thirty Years' War. In the opposite camp was the flower of the French nobility, which for splendid military qualities has never in any age or country been surpassed. The commanders were, in the highest military sense, representative men. Mercy belonged to the greatest school of German generals, and was himself unrivalled in the thoughtful skill which used to the utmost advantage the stubborn valour of his troops. Enghien excelled all French generals in rapid insight, in heroic daring, and in the faculty of kindling and keeping alive in his men the "French fury" to which the martial renown of his nation is so largely due. And, if his rash genius was to some extent sustained by the calm science of Turenne; on the other hand, the caution of Mercy was stimulated and rendered fruitful by the brilliant audacity of John of Werth.

The German army occupied a small plain on the summit of a mountain, three sides of which were thickly wooded, and surrounded by still loftier eminences shaggy with dense forests. The fourth side had a gentler slope, which was clothed with vineyards, and broken by low walls and *abattis* of felled wood; these, as well as the fortifications that crowned its crest, were held in force by Mercy's troops. On the left of the position, a deep and narrow defile wound through the wooded heights. The mouth of this ravine was strongly barricaded, and its steep sides afforded cover to bodies of picked marksmen. The rear of the German camp rested on the town of Fribourg. Turenne, judging this entrenched post to be impregnable, urged Enghien to turn it and compel the Germans to evacuate it by cutting off their supplies. But the young Duke, listening only to the suggestions of his courage, resolved, in order to retrieve the honour of the French arms, to carry it by storm. He directed Turenne, with part of the army, to force the defile and take the enemy in flank; while he, with the remainder, assailed him in front.

In order to allow time for Turenne to execute his circuitous movement, the attack was deferred until about five o'clock in the afternoon of the 3rd of August. The main body of the French climbed the mountain, through the vineyards, under a terrible fire; carried obstacle after obstacle with the greatest heroism; and reached the entrenchment on the summit. But here, worn out by the previous struggles, and disheartened by the formidable appearance of the works before them, they wavered and fell back. Enghien galloped to the front, threw himself from his horse, put himself at the head of the regiment of Conti, and flinging his baton of command into the midst of the Bavarian camp, led his men to the assault.

Inspired with resistless ardour, by the example of their general, they carried the redoubt, after frightful carnage; and when the night closed in, were masters of the enemy's last line of defence. In the meantime Turenne had been slowly winning his way against almost insuperable obstructions. Just as decisive results were about to reward his efforts, darkness, ushered in by torrents of rain and a furious storm, compelled him to pause. The French generals, uncertain of the extent of each other's progress, impatiently awaited the morning light to renew the conflict. But when day broke they discovered that their skilful antagonist, under cover of the tempestuous night, had quietly withdrawn his army to a still stronger position on the Black Mountain behind the town.

The following day, the 4th of August, was spent by the French in recovering from their fatigues, and by the Germans in completing their defences. On the 5th, as Enghien was engaged with Turenne in making dispositions for a second attack, another of his officers, Baron Espenan, disconcerted all his plans by commencing the action without orders. The fight was maintained the whole day with extraordinary obstinacy, but in the end the French were repulsed on all sides with prodigious slaughter. The heaps of dead and dying that covered the field, recklessly sacrificed in ill-judged assaults, filled the humane heart of Turenne with grief. But Enghien, with the selfish levity and the contempt for human suffering which have left the darkest blot upon his fame, jestingly remarked that "one night of Paris would repair the loss." His force, however, was so much weakened that, after watching the German position for three days, he prepared to follow the original advice of Turenne, and by making a detour, cut off his antagonist from Wurtemburg. But Mercy penetrated his designs; and fearing to be starved among the mountains, sacrificed his artillery and baggage, and withdrew his army with little loss through the passes of the Black Forest.

Though the glory of this series of desperate battles, known as the three days of Fribourg, was equally shared by the hostile generals and armies, all the solid advantages fell to the French. Within a few weeks after, Phillipsburg, Worms, Oppenheim, Mayence, Landau, Manheim and other important places surrendered to Enghien or Turenne; and then the Duke returned to the dissipations of Paris, leaving the chief command in Germany with his able lieutenant.

Enghien's sojourn in the capital during the winter of 1644-5 was marked by a violent attachment he conceived for Madamoiselle Vigean, a young lady distinguished by good sense and mental accomplishments rather than by beauty. Her virtue being proof against his solicitations, he formed the extravagant project of repudiating his wife and elevating the new object of his passion to the vacant dignity. The scheme was betrayed by Madame de Longueville to the Prince of Condé, who, greatly enraged, used effectual means to nip it in the bud. So violent, however, was Enghien's passion that when compelled to part from Mdlle. Vigean by the renewal of hostilities in the spring of 1645, he is said to have swooned away from grief.

The year 1645 opened with signal disgrace for the French arms in Germany. Turenne, after Enghien's departure, had obtained several important advantages; but while in winter quarters at Mariendal, he suffered himself to be surprised by Count Mercy and John of Werth, who destroyed or captured nearly his entire army, and all its baggage, guns, and military chest. Never was there seen more complete discomfiture. Turenne, without losing heart, applied himself, with the patient energy and the fertility of resource in which he excelled all other generals of his time, to repair this great disaster; but before he could collect the means of striking a blow the French Government again sent Enghien to supersede him in the command. The Duke brought with him a reinforcement of eight thousand men, and used every artifice to draw the enemy into a decisive battle. But the great Bavarian General, having selected a position on the plains of Nordlingen, with the tactical judgment in which he had no superior, and carefully fortified it, would only fight on his own ground.

Two hills arise, at a short distance from each other, out of the plain; one, rather precipitous, was called the Weinberg; the other had a gentler slope, and was crowned by the old Castle of Allerheim. At the entrance of the narrow valley that divided them, nestled the village of Allerheim. Mercy had drawn up his infantry in three lines across the mouth of the valley, and protected them with strong entrenchments. His right wing, under General Glen, held the Weinberg. The Imperialist cavalry, under John of Werth, was massed on his left around the Castle of Allerheim. Extensive works covered every assailable point of the position, which, formidable by nature and art, and defended by fifteen thousand excellent troops, seemed to defy attack. Enghien had only eighteen thousand men. His infantry were inferior both in numbers and quality to that of his opponent, and Turenne strove earnestly to dissuade him from hazarding an engagement on such unequal terms. But confident in his genius and fortune, and having no hope of enticing Mercy to less disadvantageous ground, the Duke drew up his army for battle. He directed Turenne with the left wing to carry the Weinberg, while Marshal Grammont with the right wing opposed John of Werth, and the Count of Marsin, with the centre, assailed the village of Allerheim. A strong force of horse and foot was stationed in the rear, under the Count of Chabot, as a reserve.

The French infantry under Marsin attacked the village, which was the key of the German position, with great fury, and succeeded in penetrating into the main street. But from the houses on either side, from the church steeple, and from the loop-holed walls of the cemetery, the Bavarian musketeers poured on them a murderous fire. Marsin fell badly wounded. His division, maintaining the struggle to the last with unavailing gallantry, was almost annihilated; and fresh regiments sent to its support under the Marquis of la Moussaye shared the same fate. Then Enghien led up the remainder of his infantry, in person, to restore the battle. Mercy, who till now had been calmly watching the progress of the fight, could not

restrain his joy on seeing Enghien's movement.
"God," he cried, "has turned the heads of the
Frenchmen; they are rushing to defeat;" and putting himself at the head of his reserves he advanced
to repel this new assault. The combat now raged
with ten-fold fury; the carnage was horrible.
The rival generals, carried away by emulation,
fought in the *mêlée* within a hundred yards
of one another. Enghien had two horses killed
under him, and three wounded; his hat and
clothes were riddled with bullets, and he was
slightly wounded in the thigh and arm. He
did all that the energy and valour of one man
could accomplish; but he had attempted impossibilities. The wrecks of his infantry, swept back
from the village by the Bavarian onset, broke and
fled in wild confusion. Mercy was killed in the
moment of victory, cheering on his troops; but
the French centre was utterly destroyed.

Meanwhile the fate of the day in other parts of
the field had been hardly less adverse to Enghien.
John of Werth, charging down from the Castle
of Allerheim, routed the right wing of the French,
and took Marshal Grammont prisoner. He then
fell on the reserve, defeated and dispersed it,
killed its commander, Chabot, and, hurried away
by the ardour of pursuit, chased the fugitives for
miles over the plain. On the left wing, Turenne

had partly scaled the Weinberg, but was held in check by General Glen. Nothing could be more unpromising than the prospect that presented itself at this moment to Enghien. The right centre and reserve of his army were gone; and the left, clinging with difficulty to the side of a steep hill, was in momentary danger of being hurled back by superior numbers, or taken in the rear. Even an able general, in such circumstances, might well have limited his plans to the saving from destruction of the still unbroken remnant of his forces.

But far different was the conception that occurred to the daring genius of the Duke. There was still left to him a small body of Hessian infantry, and a handful of cavalry. Putting himself at the head of these, he charged up the Weinberg and threw himself on Glen's men, already fully occupied by the attack of Turenne. The Germans, shaken by the impetuosity of this sudden onslaught, gave ground. Enghien pressed on, resistless; flung them down into the valley in headlong flight, and, following on their track, dispersed them completely, and took their general prisoner. He then surrounded the village of Allerheim. The victorious Bavarian infantry, deprived of their leader, and bewildered by the sudden turn of the battle, surrendered without a

blow. When, a few moments later, John of Werth returned, in all the confidence of assured success, to complete the destruction of his foes, he found the battle irretrievably lost. Never was there seen such a triumph of happy fortune and inspired audacity. Had Mercy lived, had John of Werth returned by a shorter route, had the Bavarians defended Allerheim, nothing could have saved the French from a terrible defeat. And no other general but Enghien could have plucked victory from such complete discomfiture. Napoleon, in his military criticisms, while censuring severely the temerity of the French commander in attacking such a position with forces so inadequate, has expressed the warmest admiration of his conduct in the fight. It was in reference to Enghien's heroic pertinacity, in persevering with his left wing at Nordlingen, after the rest of his army had been swept away, that the great Emperor used the following memorable words :—
"The glory and honour of his country's arms ought to be the first and highest consideration with a general who engages in battle. The safety and preservation of the army is only the second. But it is also in that same audacity and obstinacy, which the honour and glory of his country's arms demand, that the safety and preservation of the army is found. In a retreat, besides the honour

of his country's arms, he will often lose more than in two battles—a reason *never* to despair while brave men remain around the standards. By this, victory is obtained; by this, it is merited."

So great was the slaughter of the French at Nordlingen that for several days Enghien could not collect fifteen hundred infantry. Count Mercy was buried on the field of battle. The inscription on his tomb was not unworthy of the warrior—" *Sta Viator : heroem calcas.*"

This was also the last battle of John of Werth, who retired from it unmolested with his victorious horsemen. He was the most brilliant and enterprising of all the great German soldiers of his time. As a leader of cavalry, he had no equal. Like Gassion, he owed nothing to birth or fortune; his great qualities alone had raised him from the ranks of the Imperialist army to the highest command. He was especially famous for the daring and success with which he effected surprises. The secresy and skill of his plans were only matched by the force and rapidity of his blows. More than one hostile general's reputation was shattered; more than one hostile army was aroused from false security to utter destruction by the irresistible onset of John of Werth, falling like a thunderbolt out of a clear sky. And his splendid talents were enhanced by a purity of character and a lofty disinterestedness which shone brighter from being placed in contrast with the spirit of rapine and the lawless brutality so conspicuous in most of the renowned commanders of his age and country.

When he had sufficiently rested and reorganised his shattered forces, Enghien laid siege to Heilbronn; but the fatigues and excitement he had undergone induced a brain-fever which brought him to the brink of the grave. He was carried in a litter to Phillipsburg, and profusely bled, under which treatment he recovered slowly, and was unable to take any further part in the campaign. Illness and loss of blood had the effect of extinguishing his passion for Mlle. Vigean. The burning ardour of his addresses to her during the previous winter sank, on his return to Paris, at once, without any premonitory gradations, to repelling coldness; and in her grief and chagrin at this unlooked-for fickleness, she retired into a convent and took the veil.

All parties in Germany were now thoroughly exhausted by the fierce warfare which had desolated the land for more than a quarter of a century; and the negotiations for a general peace, which had been prosecuted fitfully at Munster since 1643, were renewed in a more earnest spirit. Hostilities languished during the year 1646, but were not interrupted. Turenne, at the head of the French army, pursued a successful career, but the campaign was not marked by any great battle.

In Flanders the Duke of Orleans, elated by the capture of Corutras in the preceding campaign, again claimed the command, and Enghien, impatient of inaction, volunteered to serve under his incapable cousin. His bold schemes of conquest were unpalatable to the timid mind of the Lieut.-General, and the army sat down before Mardyke. The young Duke was the soul of the operations, pressing the siege with extraordinary vigour, and courting danger at every opportunity with his usual recklessness. On one occasion, having passed the whole night in the trenches, he was refreshing himself in his tent with a party of friends, when an alarm was given that the garrison had made a sally, slaughtered the French gunners, and destroyed the works. Enghien, without waiting to put on his armour, rushed forth, followed by his companions, and attacked the enemy sword in hand. He must inevitably have been killed or taken had not Bussy Rabutin galloped up to his assistance with his company of light horse. Bussy found him laying about him with fury, and covered with the blood of his foes. The Spaniards were ultimately driven back into the town, but not until they had made prodigious havoc amongst the young French nobility.

The Spanish generals in the Netherlands, having at length drawn together their forces, advanced with confidence to raise the siege, despising the incapacity and irresolution of the Duke of Orleans. But hardly had the hostile army appeared before the French lines when it vanished, unaccountably, in the night. Enghien next morning followed in pursuit, and having with his own hand captured a young Spanish officer, demanded of him the cause of this sudden retreat. The Spaniard, wholly unsuspicious of the rank of his captor, answered simply that the Spanish commanders had heard that the Duke of Enghien was in the French camp. Mardyke, being thus abandoned to its fate, surrendered; and Orleans, satiated with victory, returned to flaunt his laurels before the admiring eyes of the good citizens of Paris. So intoxicated was this vain prince with his achievement in this and the preceding campaigns — achievements chiefly attributable to the assistance of Marshal la Meillerai and Enghien — that, quite unconscious of the ridicule provoked by such a comparison, he assumed the glorious surname which the admiration of antiquity had conferred on the son of Antigonus, and signed his letters Gaston Poliorcetes.

The capture of Dunkirk had long been an object of ardent desire to the French nation, but the difficulties of the enterprise had hitherto deterred any French general from attempting it. No sooner, however, was Enghien free to act for himself, than he marched against the place. Notwithstanding the apparently insuperable obstacles, natural and artificial, that impeded his operations, the efforts of two Spanish armies, each equal in strength to his own, and the gallant resistance of the garrison, by skill and patience he compelled the city to surrender. The news was received in Paris with joy and wonder. "I think," wrote Voiture to him, "if you undertook it you would catch the moon with your teeth." This important conquest brought the campaign of 1646 to a close.

The course of this year had wrought a momentous change in Enghien's position. During the summer his brother-in-law, the Duke of Brezé, whom Cardinal Richelieu had made High Admiral of France, was killed in a naval engagement off the coast of Tuscany. Enghien immediately claimed the post, and his pretensions were supported by the whole influence of his family. But weighty considerations, public and private, determined the Government to refuse his demand. The House of Condé already engrossed a dangerous

share of authority in the kingdom. The old
prince, besides his governments of Burgundy and
Berri, held the offices of President of the Council
and Grand Master, together with various minor
appointments conferring emolument and power.
The Duke, his son, was Governor of Champagne,
possessed the strong frontier town of Stenay, and
was the idol of the army. To confer on a young
warrior, whose ardent genius would even now
scarcely brook the slightest control, and who was
so near the throne, the supreme command of all
the sea forces of the country, would be a fatal
blunder on the part of the Regent. Moreover, Cardinal Mazarin meant to use the great
office now vacant, at once to fortify his political
position, and to promote his schemes of family
ambition. He contemplated a close alliance with
the House of Vendôme, which stood at the head of
the party of the great nobles with which he was at
variance. A matrimonial union between the young
Duke of Mercœur, heir of Vendôme, and one of
his nieces, was the object of his secret aspirations;
and the splendid dower of Admiral of France
would bridge over the social chasm that separated
the daughter of an obscure Italian gentleman from
the grandson of Henry IV. In order to soften as
much as possible her denial of Enghien's request,
Anne of Austria announced her intention of as-

suming to herself the vacant post, under the title of Superintendent of the Seas. But the resentment which the refusal called forth from the whole family of Condé was none the less violent. The Duke stormed and pressed his demand with intemperate urgency; and Condé, irritated out of his usual prudence, used menacing language, and withdrew in high anger to his Government of Burgundy. The Regent met this outburst with spirit; but Mazarin quailed, and by submissive entreaties induced Condé to return to Court in order to negotiate an arrangement. Three days after his arrival at Chantilly the old Prince died. Although not distinguished either for shining talents or for integrity of character, his death at this conjuncture was a public calamity. France could have better spared a far greater man. His clear and penetrating intellect, his long experience, his great sagacity, even the selfishness which rendered him cautious, the authority which his rank, wealth, and knowledge of the business of the State gave him, and above all the restraining influence which he alone exercised over his fiery and wayward son, would have been invaluable to the government in the stormy times that were fast approaching. Starting in life a dependent on the bounty of Henry IV., he left to his successor an income of one million livres—enormous in that age. Anne of Austria had conferred on him the vast possessions of the House of Montmorenci, forfeited to the Crown at the execution of the last Duke in 1632. If the portrait we have of him from the pen of Madame de Motteville, as he figured at the Court of the Regent, ugly and uncleanly, with red eyes, matted beard and greasy hair, at all corresponds with his appearance in his youth, there is some excuse for the unconjugal bearing of the fair Charlotte of Montmorenci. Indeed, the Marchioness of Rambouillet used to say that the princess only passed two happy days with her husband—the day of her marriage, which raised her to a place in the royal family of France, and the day of his death, which restored to her liberty.

The Queen and Cardinal Mazarin, in order to remove all traces of dissatisfaction from the mind of the new Prince of Condé, and to bind him completely to their interests, hastened to anticipate and to surpass in lavish concessions his reasonable expectations of Court favour. He was made Captain-General of the Armies of France, and invested at once with all the offices and employments held by his father, with the single stipulation that he should discontinue his opposition to the arrangement which left unfilled the place of High Admiral. The Government of Champagne was given to his younger brother, the Prince of

Conti. Condé, at the age of twenty-five, was not only the most renowned personage, but the most powerful subject in Europe, with unbounded opportunities of achieving all greatness to which the legitimate ambition of a subject can aspire. But though at first evidently overcome by the unexpected generosity of the Regent, he did not long remain satisfied. Extravagant projects of personal ambition began to fill his mind. Continually followed by the flower of the young French nobility, who imitating on all occasions the haughty bearing and imperious manners of their chief, obtained the nickname of Petits Maitres, now used to express very different qualities; seeing his boldest enterprises crowned by fortune, and his will a law to all around him, subjection even in its lightest and most splendid form was becoming irksome to him. He proposed to Mazarin to conquer Franche Compté, then a Spanish province, at his own charge, and retain it as an independent sovereignty. But the Cardinal, knowing well that the Prince would be a far more dangerous neighbour to Louis XIV. than the King of Spain, evaded compliance. This refusal led to renewed bickerings, which went on increasing in bitterness till Condé was induced, in the spring of 1647, to take the command of the French army in Catalonia, where two generals of distinction, Marshal la Mothe Houdincourt and the Count of Harcourt, had lately met with signal reverses.

Many of the leading incidents of the Prince's operations this year are recorded with inimitable felicity in the lively memoirs of Count Grammont, who with many other brilliant and dissolute Petits Maitres, accompanied their leader into Spain. When Condé arrived at Barcelona, the citizens, seeing a youth with long hair, simply attired in black, did not conceal their contempt. It became a general subject of complaint amongst them that the French Government had sent them a student and not a general. But when after a few days the Prince rode forth through the city magnificently dressed and followed by a splendid suite, they at once recognised the hero, and received him with the utmost enthusiasm. He found his army in a deplorable state of inefficiency, in want of food, ammunition, and the means of transport. Nevertheless, he marched without delay against the town of Lerida, which had lately repulsed the Count of Harcourt from its walls, with disgrace.

Lerida, the Ilerda of the Romans, looking on the country which was the scene of Julius Cæsar's celebrated campaign against the lieutenants of Pompeius, was not a place of great strength.

But the Spaniards have always, even in their most degenerate days, been formidable behind stone walls; and the town had for its commander Don Gregorio Brito, an old Portuguese officer of somewhat whimsical character, but of rare merit. The French general, filled with presumption on account of so many victories, and despising the place and its old-fashioned governor, began the siege with an insolent display which would have ill become its triumphant close. He opened the trenches in person, at the head of his own regiment, to the music of twenty-four violins; and afterwards passed the evening in revelry amidst the works. Brito made no sign until night had fallen; then sallying forth under cover of a terrific fire from the cannon on the ramparts, he swept the trenches, destroyed the labours of the French engineers, and drove back the besiegers in confusion to their camp. The next morning he sent his crest-fallen antagonist a complimentary message, with a present of iced fruit, regretting his inability to return the serenade in consequence of his want of violins, but assuring the Prince that if the music he had provided the night before had proved agreeable, he would endeavour to keep it up so long as the French did him the honour to remain before Lerida. The eccentric Portuguese was a man of his word. He did not leave the besiegers a moment's repose, and repulsed all their assaults with fearful slaughter. His vigorous sallies, the rocky nature of the soil, the want of proper engineering tools, and other necessary supplies, protracted the siege until the tardy approach of a Spanish army, and the scorching heat of summer, with its train of diseases, forced even Condé, almost beside himself with rage and chagrin, to resign all hope of success. When the relieving force of the Spaniards appeared, he drew off his troops, sadly reduced by sickness and the sword. His reverse, the first he had yet experienced, was bitterly mortifying to him, especially when he learned that the wits of Paris were diverting themselves at his expense. People had been so accustomed to consider him invincible, that his defeat was magnified far beyond its real importance, and his reputation suffered in proportion. He tried every expedient to bring the Spanish general to a battle, but the latter prudently kept his men in a strong position, protected by the guns of Lerida. Indeed, it is said that the King of Spain never wrote to him without adding as a postscript, " Above all things take good care never to engage in battle with that presumptuous youth." The campaign ended without any other military event worthy of note.

It was during the siege of Lerida that the famous,

or rather infamous, revel of La Valliere furnished a horrible picture of the reckless and ferocious gaiety of the young French nobles. The Chevalier of la Valliere, a Marechal de Camp of high lineage, being on duty, in the beginning of June, at the quarters of Marshal Grammont, invited the celebrated Bussy Rabutin, and three other young officers, named Brabantane, Breteche and Jumeaux, to dine with him at the mouth of the trenches. Seeking relief from the tedium of camp life, the guests assembled some hours before the appointed time. Breakfast was served to them, and the Prince's band enlivened the repast with military music. The part of the trenches where they were, pierced through the walls of an old church-yard. Brabantane and Breteche, moved by a diabolical spirit of pleasantry, entered through the breach, tore off the stone cover of one of the tombs, and dragging forth a recently buried corpse, wrapped in its grave-clothes, made it dance to the sound of the violins. After amusing themselves in this way for some time, their companions prevailed on them to restore the dead body to its resting-place. The party passed several hours after dinner in what Bussy Rabutin acknowledges to have been a great debauch, singing the ribald songs, compounded of blasphemy and licentiousness, then in vogue at Paris. In the midst of the Bacchanalian uproar the Marquis of la Trousse arrived to go the round of the works with La Valliere before relieving him at his post. The latter started up, telling his friends not to disturb themselves as he would return immediately. La Trousse was accustomed, in a spirit of bravado which he mistook for heroism, to walk on the outside of the trenches, and thus expose his person, without any rational object, to the enemy's fire. La Valliere, not to be out-done in folly, followed his companion's example, and had hardly gone a few paces when his skull was shattered to pieces by a ball. His guests, quite unmoved by the news, continued their revel, with the exception of Jumeaux, who rushed off to ask the Prince for a post that had been held by his friend. The incidents of this revolting banquet, almost incredible as they appear to us, would not at that period have challenged particular notoriety, had not the calamities that overtook most of the actors in the hideous scene, and the popular belief that the outraged remains were the body of a saint, awakened unusual curiosity and horror. The conduct of the officers does not, however, appear to have been made a subject of official comment, or to have elicited any mark of disapprobation from Condé or the Regent.

The check he met with before Lerida did not tend to soothe the irritation which the Prince had cherished against Cardinal Mazarin on account of imaginary grievances; and the destitute condition of the French army in Spain, which had been a main cause of his ill-success, furnished him with a juster ground of anger. His complaints on his return to Court were loud and vehement; but his support was too necessary to the government in the difficulties and dangers that now beset it, to permit the Regent or the Minister to show offence at his language. Mazarin, bending as was his wont before the storm, strove to propitiate his imperious protector by flatteries and submission, and by straining to the utmost, in desperate expedients, the crippled resources of the monarchy in order to place the army of Flanders, which Condé chose for himself, on an efficient footing for the campaign of 1648.

The position of France was now extremely critical. A long and costly war, and a corrupt administration, had ruined the finances and impoverished the people; and ill-advised measures of taxation had aroused an opposition in the capital formidable for its character and its strength, and every day growing in influence and intensity. The government could no longer obtain the most needful supplies. The State was threatened with paralysis. And during Condé's absence in Spain, the Archduke Leopold had carried everything before him on the Flemish frontier. He was now preparing to invade Picardy at the head of a well-appointed army. A decisive victory could alone avert from France the disgrace of invasion, or a humiliating peace.

Condé, having generously advanced out of his own revenues the funds required to complete the equipment of his army, set out to oppose the Archduke, who lay with eighteen thousand men, including the veteran bands of the despoiled Duke of Lorraine, on the borders of Picardy. But hardly had the first movements of the campaign begun, when Anne of Austria recalled him to Paris to advise her how to resist the urgent demands of the Parliament. During his absence Leopold entered France, and having published an insulting manifesto offering a reward for the discovery of the French army, sought for everywhere in vain and supposed to be lost, laid siege to the town of Lens. Condé hastened back with fourteen thousand men and eighteen guns, to relieve the place, but only arrived to see it surrender to the enemy, who then took up a strongly entrenched position under its walls. The Archduke calculated that the impetuous temper of his antagonist would impel him, notwithstanding his inferiority in numbers, to assault the Spanish lines. But Condé had not fought the desperate battles of Fribourg and Nordlingen, and been repulsed with disgrace from the walls of Lerida, without learning the prudence which had alone been wanting to him of the qualifications of a consummate general. Instead of the rash tactics, hardly redeemed by extraordinary genius from the reproach of foolhardiness, which had marked his previous campaigns, he put in practice a manœuvre, not more bold than masterly, for the purpose of enticing the enemy from his fortified camp.

Breaking up his own encampment in open day, he retired slowly over the undulating plain which stretched away from Lens, and which he had carefully studied. Marshal Grammont led the French van; the Prince followed with the main body, and the Marquis of Noirmoutier, with a strong force of cavalry, brought up the rear. On seeing the retrograde movement of the French, General Beck, with the troopers of Lorraine, issued from the Spanish lines to harass their retreat, and charging the rear guard, threw it into disorder. Reinforcements arrived for Noirmoutier, but Beck, also supported from his own side, continued to gain ground, till at length the Archduke, thinking the decisive moment had come for destroying the whole French army, advanced with all his forces into the plain. Meanwhile Condé had drawn up his infantry and artillery upon a gentle eminence, and had sent orders to Grammont to return at full speed. In order to release his rear guard, now sorely pressed, and to gain time for the Marshal to come up, he charged the enemy in person at the head of all his remaining cavalry. But one of those unaccountable panics, to which even the best troops are subject, seizing his men while in full career, they suddenly wheeled round and galloped back to seek shelter behind their guns. The Archduke and Beck followed up their advantage with such vigour that, notwithstanding the firm bearing of Condé's infantry and gunners, and his own desperate efforts to rally the fugitives, the battle was almost lost, when Grammont appeared. Then the fortune of the day turned. The Marshal, charging with his usual impetuosity, checked the victorious progress of the Lorraine horse. Condé only required a short respite to re-form his squadrons, restore their confidence, and lead them back into the fight with the martial fury which no enemy had ever yet been able to withstand. The troops of Spain and Lorraine fought with the most determined gallantry. The Archduke performed the part of an able general and a brave soldier. General Beck more than sustained his high renown; but when he fell, mortally wounded, his men, disheartened by his loss, relaxed their efforts and were driven from the field. Leopold escaped with difficulty by a precipitate flight; all his infantry, artillery, and baggage were captured. The victory of the French was the most complete of any in that age. Condé, as usual, had exposed himself to the greatest dangers. Two of his pages were killed at his side during the battle; but his greatest peril was incurred when the pursuit was over. Meeting Grammont as they both were returning in the evening to the French camp, he rode forward to embrace the Marshal. Their horses, which had been perfectly docile during the day, no sooner drew together than, as if possessed by furies, they rushed upon each other, and strove to tear each other to pieces. A timely pistol shot through the head of the Marshal's charger saved both riders from being frightfully lacerated.

The victory of Lens was the crowning glory of France in the long and exhausting struggle to which Cardinal Richelieu had challenged the house of Austria; it brought the Thirty Years' War to a close. Spain indeed, having concluded a separate truce with Holland, refused to be included in the treaty of Westphalia; but, crippled in power, and destitute of allies, her feeble and desultory efforts could not have been prolonged, had not the internal troubles of France afforded her a breathing time, and eventually enlisted in her support the most terrible of her foes. Hardly had the battle been won when Condé was summoned to lead his victorious army against the insurgent city of Paris. The Civil War of the Fronde, a conflict unique in the voluminous annals of faction, had broken out in France. In order to render it intelligible, it is necessary to pass in brief review the state of the kingdom during the reign of Louis XIII. and the earlier years of the Regency of Anne of Austria.

CHAPTER III.

THE history of the reign of Louis XIII. of France is in all important points the history of the rule of Cardinal Richelieu. The royal authority, during the first twelve years of that reign, had fallen into a state of impotency and contempt unknown, except for a short period preceding and succeeding the death of Henry III., during the previous century and a half. The relations of the great nobles of the kingdom to their sovereign bore a much nearer resemblance to the feudal anarchy that had existed before the reign of Louis XI., than to the loyal obedience which upheld the brilliant despotism of Francis I. The wars of the League had restored much of their ancient power. Henry IV., in bringing the long religious strife to a close, found it necessary to make concessions to his potent subjects, Catholic and Huguenot, which stripped the crown of a great part of its authority. At his death, Mary of Medicis, assuming the Regency during the minority of her son, a sickly boy only nine years old, dismissed Sully, Villeroi, and the other experienced ministers of her husband, and delivered the reins of government into the hands of her low-born and rapacious Italian favourite Concini, whom she created Marshal of France and Marquis of Ancre. The Princes of the blood, the great Catholic nobles, the powerful Huguenot connexion, indignant at the rule of an insolent upstart, and counselled by the discarded ministers, plunged into revolt, wrung humiliating concessions from the Regent—who sacrificed the interests of her son to her blind partiality for Concini's wife— and kept the kingdom for years in constant turmoil. No sooner was one Civil War appeased by lavish grants than another broke out in some rival interest.

At length, in the year 1617, the young King, at the instigation of a gentleman of his household, named De Luynes, who had acquired complete mastery over the feeble and suspicious mind of his sovereign by his aptitude in the childish amusements—the snaring of small birds, the carving of little shrines, the painting of little pictures, the beating of drums—in which Louis delighted, ordered Vitry, Captain of his Guards, to arrest Concini, giving special instructions for the use of force in case of resistance. Vitry was a willing and unscrupulous instrument. The bait of a Marshal's baton was dangled before his eyes by De Luynes; and without troubling himself about the formality of resistance on the part of his victim, he despatched Marshal D'Ancre in the court-yard of the Louvre. Louis, throwing up a window, applauded the deed. Vitry was made Marshal of France and Duke. De Luynes, created Duke and Peer, Prime Minister, and ultimately Constable, was endowed with the enormous wealth of the unhappy Italian, and with the matchless diamonds of the Italian's more unhappy wife, who was beheaded as a sorceress on the Place de Greve. To crown the fortunes of the aspiring favourite he espoused Marie de Rohan, only daughter of the Duke of Montbazon, then seventeen years old, the most beautiful, witty, wayward, and supremely fascinating woman of her time. His two brothers, obscure gentlemen, were also made Dukes and Peers, and obtained endowments suitable to their new rank. The queen-mother was deposed from power, and exiled to the castle of Blois.

In addition to extraordinary personal advantages, De Luynes possessed gracious manners, and a singularly amiable disposition, which disarmed envy, and won all hearts; but he was utterly destitute of the qualifications needed to cope with the evils which oppressed the State. His ambition was limited to the quiet enjoyment of the splendid position to which the royal favour had raised him, and for this end he laboured, though with only partial success, to conciliate hostile interests. His chief danger, however, arose not from any inimical combination, but from the fickleness of his sovereign. The angry disgust which, after a few years, seized the jealous, moody mind of Louis at the astonishing spectacle of sudden greatness, which was the work of his own hands, must have proved fatal to the whole family of De Luynes had not the Constable's death, at the end of the year 1621, prevented his inevitable disgrace. The post of prime minister being now vacant, Mary of Medicis resumed her old empire over the mind of her son. The first use she made of her recovered influence was to obtain, much against the King's inclinations, a seat in the Privy Council, and a Cardinal's hat for her Chancellor, Jean Armand Duplessis de Richelieu, Bishop of Luéon. Then began that extraordinary career which changed the face of France and of Europe.

Whoever would know what the genius and energy of one man can accomplish, for the power and glory of a State, should study the history of France during the twenty years' administration of

Cardinal Richelieu. In 1622 the provinces and strong towns of the kingdom were parcelled out as Governments, many of them held by hereditary tenure, among the Princes of the Blood and the high nobility, who appointed and removed all subordinate functionaries at their own pleasure. In Brittany the Duke of Vendôme, in Guyenne the Duke of Epernon, in Languedoc the Duke of Montmorenci, in Champagne the Duke of Nevers, in Burgundy the House of Lorraine-Guise, surrounded by populations attached to them by habits of obedience or feudal ties, could, from behind the walls of numerous strongholds, bid defiance to the King. In the West and South the Huguenot community claimed nearly all the rights of an independent State. They refused submission to the royal mandates until these were ratified by their own Synod, and made treaties of alliance with foreign powers upon equal terms. Many of the most potent houses in France, Rohan, La Force, Bouillon, La Tremouille, Chatillon, Sully, were still of their body. Their powerful military organisation, and the possession of fortresses of great strength, enabled them to brave with impunity the anger of the Government, which their turbulent spirit constantly provoked. It was only in the previous year that Louis and the Constable de Luynes, at the head of all the military force the Crown could muster, were repelled with disgrace from the Huguenot town of Montauban. In case of need La Rochelle gave easy access to the succours of England; and the Duke of Bouillon's independent principality of Sedan threw open France on the side of the Netherlands. In the East and South, the Spanish provinces of Franche Compté and Roussillon, and the dominions of the Duke of Lorraine, thrust like wedges through the frontier, and breaking up the integrity of the kingdom, were a perpetual menace to its security, and afforded support and refuge to malcontent nobles. Ever-recurring revolts, vexatious exactions and restrictions, paralysed industry and commerce. Innumerable feudal courts, possessing independent and conflicting jurisdictions, hampered the dispensing of justice. The roads were covered with robbers and assassins; nowhere was there any security for life or property. Even in Paris, in addition to the King's Courts, the Archbishop, the Abbess of Montmartre, the Grand Prior, the Abbot of St. Germain, and a number of noblemen exercised separate judicial rights. The safety of the capital was confided to forty-five decrepit watchmen; and crimes, at which humanity shudders, were daily perpetrated in the streets. Such was the internal condition of the kingdom. Abroad its influence was at the lowest ebb. Never had the House of Austria been more united or triumphant. The strength of the great Spanish Monarchy, though waning, was still unbroken; and its prestige was far greater than its strength. In Germany the Emperor, Ferdinand II., aided by his able ally, Maximilian of Bavaria, was acquiring a position of power and preponderance, for which Charles V. had striven in vain. France, weakened by her own internal dissensions, could only look on in impotent anger, while an absolute supremacy in Europe was passing, almost without a struggle, into the hands of her ancient foes.

It was the ambition of Cardinal Richelieu to bring into subjection the unruly forces that distracted the kingdom, and make them elements of national strength; to build up from the chaotic materials of antiquated feudalism a powerful and united monarchy, which might dispute the supremacy of the house of Austria in Europe. Few men ever were gifted in a more eminent degree with all the qualifications of a great ruler. He had splendid genius, prescient and fruitful, capable of conceiving and elaborating the most stupendous designs; a judgment which was never dazzled by chimerical schemes; energy and resolution to which nothing was impossible. Modest, supple, affable, haughty, stern, unrelenting, according to circumstances, he seemed to combine in himself a variety of characters; to be able to summon up at his will the most opposite qualities in aid of his ambition. Nothing was too vast, nothing too minute, for the grasp of his intellect. No circumstance, which had even a remote bearing on his policy, was too insignificant for his care. While transacting all the more important business of a great kingdom seething with agitation, and involved in complicated foreign relations, and at the same time personally directing an arduous campaign, he could find time to pen elaborate instructions for the guidance of some newly-appointed Court official. Clear-sighted in his aims, he pursued them with inexhaustible fertility of resource and unfaltering determination. As has been remarked by Bussy Rabutin, a competent and contemporary observer, from whom the foregoing estimate of Richelieu's capacity and character has been largely borrowed, it is difficult, when gazing on the noble features lit up by refined intellect and gracious benignancy which still live on the canvas of Philippe de Champagne, to understand his terrible reputation. In truth, he was by nature mild and placable. But the imperious necessities of his policy; the unscrupulous plots of princes and nobles, in concert with the foreign enemies of the realm, against his power and life, for selfish ends; the treachery and ingratitude with which his benefits were so often repaid; and doubtless, in some measure, the fierce passions which wait upon a perilous career of triumphant ambition, led him occasionally to temper justice with an exceptional severity, which wore the odious complexion of tyranny. With the doubtful exception, however, of the Duke of Montmorenci, whose life was justly forfeited for open rebellion, supported by foreign powers, there is not one of the so-called victims of Richelieu whose character or designs deserve the slightest sympathy. Nor were any of his acts tainted with the perfidy and ingratitude which marked the conduct of Henry IV. and Sully towards the Duke of Biron.

It is curious to note how sectarian prejudice brands as crime in the great Cardinal what it lauds as virtue in the great Huguenot Duke. Historians who extol to the skies the wisdom and patriotism of Sully depict Richelieu in the darkest colours as a tyrannical oppressor. Yet the policy of the two ministers was essentially identical. The depression of the great nobles and the Huguenot league at home, the depression of the house of Austria abroad, were the cherished aims of Sully—great noble, and Huguenot though he was—as they afterwards became the cherished aims of Richelieu. Both ministers laboured for the same ends; the difference was that the second brought to the work a far bolder genius and a stronger will.

If Richelieu was a redoubtable enemy, he was the most constant and generous of friends. For ability and devotion in his service, he thought no praise excessive, no recompense too splendid. And his government had one characteristic which distinguishes it honourably, not only from all contemporary governments, but from the governments of all other leading States of Europe down to quite recent times. This was the entire absence of religious intolerance. A devout believer in the creed of the Church, in which he held exalted rank, and in an age when religious animosities were running high, he knew no distinction of belief in the service of the State. He made war on the Huguenots, not as a dissenting sect, but as a political community, possessed of exceptional privileges which they abused to the detriment of the kingdom. The use he made of their complete subjugation was to place them in all respects on an equal footing with the Catholics. The Dukes of Bouillon and Schomberg and General Gassion commanded French armies under his administration, and the last two enjoyed his entire confidence. It is a striking satire upon the value of the claims to our admiration advanced most boldly by writers of eminence on behalf of communities of men, and accepted by these communities themselves with the most complacent confidence ; a curious example of the irony of history, that the principle of religious freedom, which Protestant nations always made their peculiar boast, and almost always repressed by cunning systems of savage intolerance, one of which, framed by the most powerful and free of them all, has been described by a great Protestant writer, as "more terrible than the ten Christian persecutions," was practised in Catholic France alone, during that part of the seventeenth century when the kingdom was absolutely governed in succession by a French and an Italian Cardinal, Richelieu and Mazarin.

Richelieu only shares the common fate of all great men who have been successful, and whose careers have brought them into collision with powerful interests, in having his merits depreciated by envy, and his defects exaggerated by malignity. There is nothing, perhaps, in history which gives a more painful shock to a generous mind than the revelation of the infirmities of a glorious spirit, of petty and degrading feelings harboured in a lofty soul; except it be the hideous joy with which baser natures gloat over and distort failings which disfigure natures, in other respects God-like, into some resemblance to themselves. Richelieu's opponents, vanquished in political strife, have taken a dastardly revenge for his superiority in their memoirs. It may freely be admitted that neither as a statesman nor as a man was he by any means perfect. The irregular grandeur of his character cast gigantic shadows. As a ruler, his policy struck not only at excessive privileges, but at legitimate rights; its tendency was to crush political freedom as well as anarchy. It may be said in extenuation that this is the fault of strong governments in periods of disorder and transition; that considering the times and the country in which he lived, and the work he had to accomplish, it was almost inevitable; that anarchy is more fatal to liberty than tyranny itself. He was one of the most generous and enlightened patrons of men of genius; one of the most zealous fosterers of literature and the fine arts that ever lived; yet his treatment of the illustrious Corneille seems to have been inspired by resentments of jealous vanity which would have dishonoured a starving poetaster, which betray kinship with the meanest passions of his countryman, Voltaire. The amusing story in the Memoirs of the Count of Brienne, in which the powerful minister is described as having been beguiled by Madame de

Chevreuse into dancing a saraband in appropriate trappings of green velvet, castanets, and silver bells, in order to win the love of Anne of Austria; and the equally circumstantial accounts of his midnight interviews in masquerade with the celebrated Marion de L'Orme, would seem to show that he discarded alike personal dignity and professional decency in the pursuit of pleasure. But it must in fairness be taken into account, that these anecdotes emanate from his deadly enemies at one of the most corrupt and unscrupulous periods of modern history; that they did not appear till after his death, when authoritative contradiction had become impossible; and that they all want impartial confirmation. Anne of Austria, in her unreserved revelations, many years afterwards, to Madame de Motteville, of the incidents of her married life, does not appear to have known anything of the story of the saraband. With every deduction which justice can claim on account of errors and shortcomings, Richelieu will ever rank among the master spirits of the world; and of the many illustrious public men who have adorned France, and who were strictly Frenchmen, there are few indeed who can boast a purer, not one who can boast a more splendid fame.

The difficulties inherent to the gigantic task, which Richelieu set himself to accomplish, were aggravated by weakness or perverse opposition in quarters from which he might naturally have expected the most strenuous support. Louis XIII., shy, ill-educated, consumed by morbid melancholy, deeply but gloomily religious, a prey to constantly recurring fits of illness which brought him to the brink of the grave; devoted to unkingly, if innocent pursuits; incapable of governing by himself, yet sensitively jealous of the appearance of control; and easily influenced through his peculiar tastes; his smouldering impatience of political tutelage, and his conscientious scruples, could only be ruled by the nicest art and the firmest temper. There were in the Minister's favour, the King's despotic tendencies, passion for military distinction, shrinking disgust under the burthen of State cares to which he felt himself unequal, and above all the enormous faults of his own enemies. Though Richelieu soon succeeded in inspiring his Sovereign with admiration and awe, these, and not affection, formed the link that bound them together to the end.

Louis had been married at the age of fourteen, through the policy of Mary of Medicis, to Anne of Austria, eldest daughter of Philip III. of Spain, born in the same year as himself. Seldom has there been a more uncongenial union. Anne was beautiful, proud with more than traditional pride of her race and country, fond of admiration and gaiety, daring, clever, and unscrupulous. The cold temperament of her husband, his joyless mood, which found its chief solace in singing dreary ditties of his own composing, and in prolonged fits of sullen musing, filled her with disgust. Her forced subjection, first to the ascendency of De Luynes, and afterwards to the control of the Queen-mother, excited her bitter indignation. The precarious health of her husband, by constantly inspiring her with fallacious hopes of release from irksome ties, prevented her schooling her haughty humour into the submission and the show of sympathy which would have given her dominion over his mind. And after a time the unbounded influence of the brilliant and dissolute Duchess of Chevreuse fortified her rebellious spirit and corrupted her heart.

Richelieu, on assuming the direction of affairs, whether, as his detractors relate, prompted by a frantic passion, or, as is more probable, by motives of policy and good-feeling, strenuously endeavoured to win the young Queen's favour. But Anne, counselled by Madame de Chevreuse, rejected his advances with scorn, and openly proclaimed herself his foe. No sooner had his genius asserted its supremacy in the royal councils, no sooner had his policy begun to unfoldi tself, than they naturally provoked fierce, wide-spread and stubborn antagonism. As the immediate and obvious effect of his measures was to increase the authority wielded by himself, he seemed to the great majority of Frenchmen, while really working out, in the interests of France and of civilization, an inevitable political and social revolution, to be merely obeying the tyrannical impulses of an insatiable personal ambition. The great Catholic nobles, the Huguenot confederacy, the Princes of the Blood, encouraged by the open or secret support of England, Spain, and Lorraine, arrayed themselves against his projects. His old patroness, Mary of Medicis, exasperated at the independent attitude towards herself, which the responsibilities of his position compelled him to assume, conceived for him a furious hatred, which he tried in vain to appease by submission, and even by tears. In concert with her daughter-in-law she urged her younger son, Gaston, Duke of Orleans, to form leagues with foreign powers against the throne of his brother, and the life of the Minister, the scheme of the confederates comprehending the marriage of Anne and Gaston in the probable event of the King's death or deposition. Her importunities, assailing him in periods of sickness and mental prostration, wrung from Louis more than once a solemn pledge to dismiss the Cardinal from his councils. But the fortune and the indomitable will of Richelieu triumphed over all foes and all obstacles. The Huguenots, though aided by the whole power of England, saw their strongholds captured and their dangerous privileges abolished. The Princes of the Blood, and the great nobles, stripped of their governments, hereditary fiefs, and independent principalities, expiated their treason by death, outlawry, or imprisonment. Mary of Medicis, driven from France, died in exile at Cologne, in want of the necessaries of life. Gaston of Orleans, discredited by the incapacity, cowardice and treachery, that caused the destruction of his accomplices in a succession of abortive conspiracies, lost the power of doing harm. Anne of Austria having forfeited for ever the regard and respect of her husband by the scandalous levity of her conduct, her anxiety to marry his brother, and her treasonable correspondence with the enemies of the kingdom, was subjected to the most humiliating restraints, and barely escaped destruction by throwing herself on the Cardinal's mercy. With Louis himself the relations of his Minister at last bore a strong resemblance to those which had existed between the Mayors of the Palace and the degenerate Sovereigns of the Merovingian dynasty; but the blood shed in the field and upon the scaffold cemented not only the ephemeral authority of the Cardinal, but also the aggrandised and enduring authority of the House of Bourbon. Abroad, the subsidies, and afterwards the armed intervention, of France, enabled Gustavus Adolphus, and the Protestant chiefs who succeeded him in command, to crush for ever the power of the Emperor; while the conquest of Roussillon and Lorraine, the revolt of Catalonia, and the occupation of Savoy, attested the humiliation of Spain. Even the grave could not conquer the strong spirit of the great Cardinal. It ruled the councils of France long after the wasted body, its earthly tenement, worn out as a sword wears through its scabbard, had become dust. His dying wishes were more implicitly obeyed than ever was the political testament of a King of France. The statesmen whom he had formed continued after his death to direct the Government; and Cardinal Mazarin, whom on his death-bed he recommended to Louis as his successor, followed, though with unequal steps, in the political path of his master.

The character of Cardinal Mazarin, who is justly entitled to a foremost place among great modern statesmen, was cast in a very different mould from that of his illustrious predecessor. Crafty, with the deep and subtle craft of an Italian politician, wary and insinuating, rather than enterprising and bold, he trusted more to wiles than to vigorous action, and never resorted to force, for the compassing of an object, till he had exhausted all the arts of persuasion and intrigue. He was a master of all the learning and the accomplishments of the time. His knowledge of foreign politics was at once extensive and profound. He possessed rare gifts of eloquence and perspicuity in speaking and writing. Having exquisite natural taste, carefully cultivated by study and travel; being adorned in an eminent degree with personal grace and beauty, and with brilliant and agreeable qualities of mind; and blending in his manners the stately gravity due to a Spanish education, with the deferential courtesy of his Italian breeding, he had no rival in Europe as a finished diplomatist. As an adept in deceit, and in the whole dark science of state-craft, he perhaps has seldom been surpassed. But for a statesman of the so-called Machievellian school, he had two great defects. He wanted the ruthless will which marches to its goal without pity and without remorse; and he was deficient in the power of simulating honesty or of recognising that quality in others. Of a disposition gentle almost to timidity, he was apt to over-reach himself by finesse; and his habit of calculating too exclusively on the baser motives of human actions led him sometimes into fatal blunders. Intercourse with him sooner or later infallibly awakened in friend and foe an uncomfortable feeling of being cheated. Without possessing the lofty range or the force of genius that distinguished Richelieu, his mind, though liable to be clouded by self-interest and by passing fears, was remarkable for acuteness, for the prescient sagacity of its views, for marvellous fertility of resource, and for a patient tenacity of purpose irresistible as destiny itself. " Time and I against any other two" was his favourite maxim. He seldom, if ever perhaps, postponed his private ends to the good of the State, but he generally shaped them in harmony with what he believed to be the public advantage. He belonged to the school of statesmen who held, or at least acted as if they held, that peoples were made for Kings; and in the main he carried out, by a feebler and more demoralising policy, the system of Government which he inherited from his predecessor. Although under the dominion of avarice, the meanest of all vices, and in a Minister like Mazarin, with despotic principles, unbounded opportunities, and a low standard of political morality, one of the most hurtful to a people, its influence was somewhat tempered by his love of magnificence and refined enjoyments, and his splendid patronage of the fine arts. He merits the high praise of being the most clement of rulers. There is no other example in history of a minister of such insatiable ambition, guided by such arbitrary maxims, pursued and proscribed for so many years with such unscrupulous malignity, such furious rancour, and ultimately so triumphant over all his enemies, who treated his adversaries with equal forbearance, and so consistently shrank from dipping his hands in blood.

The origin of Mazarin was obscure; his father, of Sicilian extraction, having been steward in the household of the great Roman family of Colonna. The young Gulio, born in 1602, was sent for his education to the University of Alcalá, in Spain. On his return to Rome, the interest of his patrons obtained for him a commission in the Papal Army. But although he never lost his military tastes, he soon relinquished the profession of arms for a career better suited to his genius. His skill in literary composition having attracted the notice of the Cardinals Barberini, nephews of the reigning Pontiff, Urban VIII., they took him under their protection; and charmed by his versatile capacity and his amiable disposition, advanced him to important diplomatic employments in Italy and France. His new profession brought him, in the year 1630, during the Mantuan war, into contact with Cardinal Richelieu, who appreciating his great abilities and his engaging qualities, loaded him with marks of esteem and affection. Mazarin happened to be in Paris in the year 1639 on a confidential mission from the Papal See, when the sudden death of Father Joseph de Tremblay deprived Richelieu of his most able and trusted councillor. The powerful minister fixed upon the Papal Envoy as the person best qualified to supply the loss, assigned him apartments in the Palais Cardinal, obtained for him the red hat which had been destined for the famous Capuchin, and admitted him to his entire confidence. Mazarin was especially useful to his benefactor as a medium of communication with the King and Queen. His gentle pliancy, and deferential bearing, soothed the jealous and irritable temper of Louis. His insinuating manners and perfect knowledge of the Spanish tongue won him the regard of Anne of Austria, now reduced to isolation by the death or banishment of nearly all her adherents.

On the death of Richelieu the position of his followers was eminently precarious. The existence of the King had long held by a thread. It was impossible that life could flicker much longer in his emaciated frame; and his children were still infants. The statesmen of the school of the late minister, men of great ability and eager ambition, who had been absolutely devoted to their patron, not only represented a policy odious to the great body of the nation, but had in many cases excited the personal enmity of the Queen, and of the great nobles of the realm. The House of Condé, aggrandized in an extraordinary degree by its alliance with Cardinal Richelieu, was their chief support; but the character of the Prince was proverbially shifty and self-seeking. It seemed as if the political structure reared by their master with such a bold and skilful hand would topple down in ruin on their heads. Louis, even while the impression of the solemn death-bed interview which terminated the momentous, ever varying, but never-broken relations which had bound him and his great minister together for twenty years, was still fresh on his mind, had displayed singular ingratitude and want of feeling. When the Cardinal's death was reported to him, not caring to dissemble his joy at being released from the servitude which he had neither known how to throw off nor to support with dignity, he exclaimed "I am at length a king." For a few weeks he seemed to enjoy his liberty, and the appearance of directing in person the government of the kingdom. In order, apparently, to convince his subjects that the severity which had hitherto distinguished his reign was solely due to the counsels of the deceased prelate, he granted

an amnesty for political offences. Princes of the
Blood and great nobles, long entombed in dungeons, or forced to eat the bitter bread of exile,
again thronged the Royal ante-chambers at St. Germain. Every day added to the returned swarm of
illustrious proscribed, who, gathering in excited
groups, scowled with hatred and scorn at the
adherents of the late minister, decked out in the
dignities of which they had been despoiled;
watched with ill-dissembled hope the manifest
tracings of death upon the countenance of their
sovereign; and crowded in noisy homage around
Anne of Austria, their old accomplice in treason,
and the destined instrument of their triumph and
revenge. The leading figure among these haughty
malcontents was the young Duke of Beaufort,
second son of the Duke of Vendôme, and grandson of Henry IV., brave, handsome, rash, presumptuous, without capacity· or conduct, but
popular and high in the favour of the Queen.

To the dangers he shared in common with his
colleagues was added, in the case of Mazarin, the
odium nearly always provoked by the rapid elevation of a foreign adventurer of obscure extraction.
The difficulties of his situation could only be surmounted by the exercise of all his art. Policy
and his natural disposition suggested the same
course of action. He set himself to attract friends

and disarm foes, by humility of deportment, by flattering caresses, and by constant offices of kindness. Naturally inclined to luxury and magnificence, he adopted a style of living plain even to meanness. He took pains to conceal his influence in the King's councils, and affected a wish to be permitted to retire to Rome. He paid obsequious homage to rank and power, and did not disdain to propitiate the most insignificant court official. His efforts to win the favour of the Queen, though secret, were unremitting. Nor was Anne of Austria, now in the ripe splendour of her voluptuous beauty, and aspiring to be Regent with absolute power, insensible to the charm which personal graces and delicate flattery lent to the councils of the astute politician.

Within five months Louis XIII. followed Cardinal Richelieu to the grave. When he felt his end drawing near, he summoned Mazarin and Baron Chavigny, the ablest and best beloved of Richelieu's political pupils, to assist him in preparing an Edict of Regency to regulate the government of France during the minority of his son. Mazarin prudently held aloof as much as possible from the discussions in the Council of State, resigning the lead to the bolder Chavigny, by whose advice a solemn Declaration of the King's will was drawn up, and formally registered by the Parliament of Paris. To this settlement Louis exacted public oaths of obedience from his wife, from the great judicial and administrative bodies of the Capital, and from the principal personages of the realm. Ancient precedent and the necessities of the time compelled him, notwithstanding the well-founded distrust and dislike with which he regarded his wife and his brother, to appoint the one Regent and the other Lieutenant-General of the kingdom. But he vested a controlling power in a Council of Regency, composed, in addition to the Duke of Orleans, of the Prince of Condé, Mazarin, Chavigny, and his father Bouthillier, and the Chancellor Seguier.

The conduct of the Queen at this juncture was marked by all the perfidy of which her husband so often and so bitterly complained, and by a degree of political skill for which no one, with the exception perhaps of Richelieu, had hitherto given her credit. Knowing well that her own popularity, the passions of the great nobles, and the strong reaction that had already set in against the repressive system of the late minister, would sweep away the unusual restrictions imposed upon her by the King's testament, and, counselled by Mazarin to temporise, she took the required oath with cheerful alacrity, and with earnest protestations of devotion and gratitude. In order to guard herself against the cabals of the Duke of Orleans, who had publicly questioned the legitimacy of her children; and to escape from the position of being merely the head of a turbulent and rapacious faction, of dependence on her old partizans, with whose political views she no longer sympathised, she formed a secret league for mutual support with the Prince of Condé, the mainstay of Richelieu's friends, and the mortal enemy of the House of Vendôme. The event fully justified her prudence and foresight. On the death of Louis XIII., the Duke of Beaufort and his party, treating the Edict of Regency, and the Council of Regency with contempt, carried Anne in triumph to Paris, amidst the acclamations of the people, as absolute ruler of the realm. The Lieutenant-General and the Council, influenced by Condé, who had been gained over, and by Chavigny, whose sagacity divined the necessities of the situation, determined upon a voluntary abdication of their functions. In a few days Louis XIV., then five years old, held his first Bed of Justice. Orleans, with ill-dissembled reluctance, announced to the High Court of Parliament the resignation of himself and his colleagues in the Government, and proposed to invest the Regent with unlimited authority. Condé signified his approval. A decree was passed amidst the greatest enthusiasm by which the magistrates annulled the will of Louis XIII., which they had so recently affirmed with equal unanimity. Orleans was again created Lieutenant-General of the Kingdom by the Regent; and the members of the Council of Regency, with Condé as President, continued to hold their posts at her pleasure.

Anne of Austria had now attained the fruition of her hopes. But the exultation of success was soon sobered by the difficulties of her new position. She found herself between two irreconcilably hostile parties, each of which had contributed to promote her ambition. The one composed of the House of Condé, the connexions of Richelieu, the experienced statesmen and able soldiers he had raised around the throne, represented victory and the humiliation of the house of Austria abroad, and the plenitude of the royal authority at home. These urged her to recollect only that she was mother of the King of France, to observe the treaty engagements of the kingdom sealed on many a glorious field of battle, and to preserve in undiminished splendour the inheritance of her son. The other party, consisting of the majority of the great princes and nobles, her own old confederates, backed by the Church and by popular feeling, peremptorily demanded immediate peace without regard to existing alliances and public faith, with the other Catholic powers; the restoration of the forfeited dominions and feudal powers of the depressed nobles; the confiscation of Richelieu's wealth, the degradation of his family and adherents, and the reversal of his policy. The very first acts of her authority as Regent revealed to her the inevitable dangers that beset her course. On her return to the Louvre from the Palace of Justice she had appointed several of her old adherents to seats in the Council of State, and made one of them, the Bishop of Beauvais, Prime Minister. But she also commissioned a confidential agent to offer Mazarin, who since the death of the king had secluded himself in his dingy lodgings, professing to his friends ignorance of the intrigues on foot, and despondency regarding his own prospects, the post of Vice-President of the Council. And in observance of her secret engagements with Condé, an intimation was conveyed to Chavigny, Bouthillier, and the Chancellor Seguier of her desire that they should retain their offices in the Ministry. Beaufort and his friends, almost beside themselves with amazement and anger, immediately assailed her with clamorous remonstrances, which she endeavoured, with only partial success, to satisfy by representing to them the necessity of temporising until she had acquired some knowledge of public affairs. They only consented to wait until their mistress had the support of the presence and counsels of Madame de Chevreuse, whose return from her long exile in the Netherlands was daily expected, before, as they openly declared, transferring to themselves all the offices and governments which had been usurped during the late reign by the adherents of the new political system, and all the vast possessions acquired by the family of Cardinal Richelieu. The character and career of the extraordinary woman, upon whose return to Court such momentous issues seemed to hang, call for something more than a mere passing notice.

When the Duke of Luynes found himself suddenly raised from obscurity and indigence to the highest rank, and unbounded wealth, by the favour of Louis XIII. and the plunder of the unfortunate Concinis, his first care was to add lustre and strength to his new position by an alliance with one of the great families of France. The unrivalled charms, sparkling wit, and imperious spirit of Marie de Rohan, only daughter of the Duke of Montbazon, had, just then, burst upon the Court of France in a dawn which gave dazzling promise of the transcendent power which afterwards set the world in a flame. De Luynes, with the support of the King, sought Marie's hand in marriage. In order to promote his suit,

he laid at the feet of the proud young beauty the
magnificent diamonds of the Marchioness d'Ancre,
said to exceed in value those in the possession of
any other European subject, and the office of
Superintendent of the Queen's Household, the
greatest which a woman could hold under the
French Crown. The handsome person and winning manners of the favourite made an impression
on Mademoiselle de Rohan's heart; his splendid
offers dazzled her ambition, and she accepted his
hand without reluctance. But her elevation at
Court was opposed by an angry cabal. The
young Queen resisted an appointment which
placed at the head of her household a self-willed
beauty but a year older, and of more brilliant
attractions than herself. The Duchess of Montmorenci and the haughty Spanish dames who
had hitherto formed Anne's establishment, refused to acknowledge the new Superintendent, and
Louis had to exert the royal authority with some
harshness, to make his will obeyed. Marie lived
happily with her husband, and up to the time of
his death, supported his interests with the
courageous fidelity which was the finest feature of
her character. During the first year of her
widowhood, the miscarriage of Anne of Austria,
caused by a fall while romping with Madame de
Luynes in the long gallery of the Louvre, led to

the dismissal of the Duchess and her banishment from Court. A few months after her disgrace she married the Duke of Chevreuse, youngest son of Henry Duke of Guise, who had been murdered at Blois. This great alliance procured her recal to Court and her re-appointment to high office about the person of. the Queen. In other respects her second marriage was unfortunate. Chevreuse, who had degencrated from his illustrious race in everything except personal beauty, was sunk in sloth and pleasure. The Duchess, neglected by her husband, threw off all moral restraint, gave free rein to her bold and wayward spirit, and with qualifications for success which have seldom been equalled, launched out upon that stormy career of intrigue in love and politics, which soon made her the most famous woman in Europe.

The coldness which had at first existed between Anne of Austria and the young Superintendent of her household gradually gave place to feelings of confidence and affection. Madame de Chevreuse espoused the quarrels of her mistress, who keenly resented the precedence allowed to the Queen-mother by the jealous distrust of the King, with the passionate ardour of her nature. Richelieu, then rising rapidly in power, conceived for her a profound admiration which nothing was ever able to extinguish. He spared no effort to win her over to his interests. But she treated his advances with galling mockery, turned him into ridicule with the Queen, and was the soul of every conspiracy that troubled his administration. A large share of the faults and the unhappiness of Anne of Austria's married life must be attributed to the evil influence of Madame de Chevreuse. She encouraged the Queen in her ill-judged course of political cabal, and domestic contumacy. In concert with her lover, Lord Holland, she was the promoter and confidante of the Queen's liason with the Duke of Buckingham; and bore a principal part in the celebrated midnight revels in the gardens of the Louvre and at Amiens which cast dishonour on the throne of France. She was the most active member of the conspiracy of the Prince of Chalais for the assassination of Richelieu and perhaps of the King, and the marriage of Anne of Austria with the Duke of Orleans. Chalais, betrayed and deserted by Orleans and his other associates, was sustained in prison, and even to the foot of the scaffold, by her fearless devotion. Her multiplied offences naturally provoked the indignation of Louis XIII. He would have shut her up in the Bastille, but at the Cardinal's intercession, she was exiled for a few months to her chateau at Dampierre, and then permitted to retire to the Court of the Duke of Lorraine.

The Minister, however, soon found that the implacable Duchess was a more formidable foe in exile than at the Court of France. Wandering restlessly from one country to another, impelled by vanity, ambition and hatred, she compelled sovereigns and statesmen of the most opposite views and character to confess the power of her fascinations and become accomplices in her schemes. Men and women, the most virtuous and the most abandoned, alike found points of irresistible attraction in the curiously chequered nature of the brilliant Frenchwoman. Admired and fêted at the Courts of Madrid, London, Brussels, and Nancy, she raised up enemies everywhere against the French Government, and knit together powerful foreign confederacies to aid the efforts of domestic insurrection. She and her party would have seen with joy the troops of Spain and Lorraine penetrate into the heart of France from the East, while the English advanced victoriously from the Huguenot fortresses in the West, so that the successful invasion should hurl the detested Cardinal from power.

Yet in the very midst of their mortal duel it seemed as if Richelieu and Madame de Chevreuse suddenly agreed to bury their animosities and unite their interests. After the final discomfiture of the caballings of Mary of Medicis, at the very moment when she was exulting in assured success, on the memorable "Day of Dupes," the Cardinal made the Marquis of Chateauneuf Keeper of the Seals. Chateauneuf was a favoured lover of the Duchess. Delighted at his advancement, and anxious to witness his good-fortune, she offered her friendship to Richelieu. The Minister, ever willing to convert her into a friend, induced the King to permit her to return to the French Court, and to have unrestricted access to Anne of Austria. But the plots against his administration were continued without interruption; and after a time he discovered that Chateauneuf, who had given a strong proof of devotion by presiding at the trial of his early benefactor the Duke of Montmorenci, debauched by his mistress, was betraying the secrets of State to Anne of Austria, and habitually reviling himself with the grossest license of accusation and invective. The treacherous Keeper of the Seals was condemned to perpetual imprisonment, under harsh restrictions, in the citadel of Angouleme. Madame de Chevreuse was ordered to retire again to Dampierre, and strictly forbidden to hold communication with the Queen.

Nothing daunted by ill-success, she continued her intrigues with foreign powers; and journeying up to Paris disguised as a peasant-woman, held secret interviews with Anne of Austria in the Convent of Val de Grace. The spies of the Cardinal

detected these stolen visits of his fair enemy. The
Duchess was hurried away from Dampierre to a
melancholy chateau in the gloomy depths of a
vast forest near Tours; and, what she resented as
unpardonable malice on the part of the Minister,
was committed to the rigorous control of her
husband. Richelieu, however, soon relented to
her expostulations, permitted her to live at Tours,
where she completely captivated the simple old
Archbishop, and supplied her liberally with
money. She remained at Tours carrying on secret
correspondence with the Queen, and with Spain,
Lorraine, and the banished nobles, until the
detection of her treasonable intrigues by Richelieu
placed the life of Anne of Austria herself at his
mercy. Then the Duchess, justly fearing that she
had exceeded the utmost limits of forbearance,
resolved to fly the country. Leaving Tours in her
coach, as if for an afternoon drive, she attired herself in the dress of a cavalier, sent back the equipage,
with the blinds drawn down, by a circuitous route,
and mounted a horse which had been stationed at
a convenient point caparisoned for a journey. Her
splendid jewels, the bequest of her first husband,
were committed, on the road, to the charge of the
young Prince of Marsillac. Riding post, without
attendants, she traversed the southern provinces
of France, meeting with ludicrous adventures,

from which she extricated herself with peculiar gaiety and sang-froid, and finally crossed the Pyrennees in safety. But although received at the Courts of the powers hostile to France with almost regal honours, Madame Chevreuse, a true Frenchwoman, pined amidst the most splendid scenes of foreign capitals for the delights of Parisian society. After a short time, she made fresh overtures with the view of obtaining permission to return to France. The Cardinal, always indulgent to his beautiful enemy, and no longer fearing her influence over the Queen, required from her only submission, and a promise of amendment. But Anne of Austria, who now had her own reasons for dreading the presence of her restless friend, secretly contrived the means of putting a stop to the negociations.

At the time of Richelieu's death, the |Duchess had been six years in exile; years of disappointment and chagrin, which made sad havoc in the peerless charms, which thrice that period of active intrigue had touched only to improve. And the event which might have been counted on as the termination of her wanderings, seemed likely to render them eternal. Louis XIII. specially excepted her from the amnesty he granted for political offences, and by his last testament condemned her to perpetual banishment from the

French Court. When the Parliament of Paris had annulled this will, the Regent, with apparent cordiality, but real reluctance, despatched missives of recal to her old ally, then the guest of the Archduke Ferdinand, at Brussels. The Duchess and the Flemish Court, confident of her unbounded empire over the mind of Anne of Austria, and believing that her return to France would be immediately followed, notwithstanding the recent victory of Rocroi, by the entire reversal of Richelieu's political measures, publicly manifested undignified exultation. In council with her Spanish friends she mapped out the future policy of France, and accepted their premature gratitude for an advantageous peace with a gracious condescension which was untroubled by a single doubt. Departing from Brussels attended by the whole Court, welcomed along her route by the Flemish and French authorities with extraordinary public honours, she slowly pursued her triumphal progress towards Paris, disdainful of the ominous warnings transmitted to her through common friends by her irritated mistress, of the revolution which circumstances had wrought in the Regent's feelings and opinions.

It must be admitted that the party of great nobility and their foreign allies had apparently strong grounds for satisfaction at the change of government in France. Few even amongst those most experienced in the crooked ways of political life entertained a doubt as to the side to which the Regent would incline. She was known to have lent her sanction to most of the plots formed in the late reign by the feudal party, in concert with her brother the King of Spain; plots which did not always respect the crown, perhaps the life, of her husband. She was, notoriously, the bosom friend of the most active spirit of that party; and even in exile Madame Chevreuse had continued, seemingly to the very last, not only to inspire the councils of her friends, but to rule the heart of her mistress. In the long struggle for power, Anne, as she and her partizans loudly proclaimed, had received at the hands of Richelieu and his creatures not only great injuries, but insults devised with ingenious malice to outrage her feelings as a queen and a woman. She had been more than once rescued from terrible perils, provoked by her imprudence, by the self-immolating fidelity of devoted adherents. Proud of her lineage and of her beauty, imperious and self-willed, courageous even to temerity, quick and apparently tenacious in her feelings, Anne did not seem one who could find it easy to forget an obligation or an injury. It was natural that her accession to sovereign rule should make the followers of the late Minister tremble for their safety; that her tried partizans whom the prisons had disgorged, or who had flocked around her from banishment, should exult in anticipation of the signal vengeance and the splendid rewards with which the haughty daughter of the Cæsars would requite so much devotion and so many wrongs. Moreover, Anne was a Spanish Infanta, warmly attached to her brother, the Catholic King, in whose interests she had more than once betrayed her adopted country; warmly attached to the Catholic faith, although she might occasionally temper the severity of her religious principles by laxity of practice. The ties of family and religion bound her to dissolve the unholy league, which to the scandal of Christendom, a Prince of the Church had formed with heretical powers, in order to check the triumphant march of Catholicity in Germany.

But there were causes, some unsuspected at that time, some not sufficiently taken into account, which operated so as, in a great measure, to falsify the hopes and fears to which her assumption of the Regency had given birth. Her real nature was a sealed volume even to her most intimate friends. Not even the sharp-witted Duchess of Chevreuse seems to have harboured a suspicion of the strong-willed ambition and the deep duplicity which lay at the foundation of the character of the seemingly pliant beauty, so greedy of admiration, and so prone to levity, of all whose rash escapades in love and politics, of whose most secret moments she had been long the confidante. And, during the last five years of his rule, Anne, unknown to all her friends, appears to have been in intimate, though carefully concealed, alliance with Cardinal Richelieu. At that terrible juncture of her life, when the Cardinal, having discovered that his military plans were betrayed and his secret negociations foiled by her treachery, charged her with high treason in the Council of States; when the faithful agent of her political crimes, La Porte, was seized and flung into a dungeon of the Bastile, where his constancy would probably be tested by the rack; when, in an agony of despairing terror, she besought the Prince of Marsillac to carry her out of France; when the beautiful and virtuous Mademoiselle de Hautefort, throwing to the winds, with the noblest self-devotion, the love of the King, her own safety, and, what she valued far more, her reputation, in order to rescue her mistress from destruction, penetrated into the Bastile, disguised as a soubrette, to communicate with La Porte, whose heroic fidelity extorted a warm tribute of admiration from the baffled minister; and when all these efforts, and even her own wanton perjury in the Holy Eucharist were of no avail against the clear proofs in the Cardinal's possession, Anne threw herself on Richelieu's mercy, and purchased safety by unconditional submission. She continued to be the object of the ardent loyalty of her old friends, who confided to her all their plots. There is a good reason to believe it was from her the Cardinal, oppressed by the gloom of mortal illness and approaching disgrace at Tarascon, received the mysterious packet which enabled him to crush the conspiracy of Cinq Mars, and finally establish his power.

Richelieu, on his part, rendered the humiliating restrictions which Louis XIII. imposed on his wife less intolerable, and promoted her interests. Aided by a seasonable storm, which drove the King for a night's shelter to his wife's apartments in the Louvre, the only habitable portion of the Palace, he brought about a renewal of conjugal relations, which had been interrupted since the conspiracy of the Prince of Chalais. This reconciliation resulted in the birth of a Dauphin after a barren nuptial of twenty years. We have the Queen's own public testimony to the effect that had the great minister survived Louis XIII. she would, if possible, have added to his power. Mother of a king and ruler of a mighty kingdom she had no longer the views and interests of the neglected childless wife, encompassed by the creatures and oppressed by the domination of a triumphant enemy. The point of most moment to her was no longer a question of persons, but a question of State policy; not so much whether one of two rival factions should prevail, as whether the absolute authority of the King should be established on the wrecks of the feudal system, or the over-grown power of the nobles should again overshadow the throne. And it required a very short experience of governing to teach her that to break with the experienced politicians of Richelieu's party would be to throw the kingdom, at a perilous crisis, into inextricable confusion. Mazarin and Chavigny held in their hands the threads of a net-work of political schemes which embraced half of Europe. They alone possessed the ability and knowledge of affairs required to steer the vessel of the State through the perils of a period of foreign war and internal transition. The feudal party, long ostracised, and for the greater part incapable, lost no opportunity of displaying equal ignorance and presumption. Their swelling self-conceit and fussy incompetency soon won for them the nickname of " The Importants." The Marquis of Chateauneuf, the only able and experienced statesman they could boast, broken by twelve years of solitary imprisonment, and proscribed by the fierce enmity of the House of Condé for the part he had played in the tragic downfall of the last Duke of Montmorenci, sought only a tranquil retreat at his country house of Montrouge. Their ostensible leader, the Bishop of Beauvais, was, in the words of Cardinal de Retz, "a mitred fool;" "an idiot of idiots." And, in addition to the disadvantages suggested by a comparison of persons, to hand over to the Importants the reins of Government would be to goad into revolt an able and powerful party, headed by the wily Condé and his heroic son, and to undo the labours of Cardinal Richelieu. Thus new motives, born of new political circumstances, had gradually estranged Anne of Austria from her old friends. Another consideration, springing from softer emotions, and perhaps equally potent, had also begun to influence her conduct. The various ability and political knowledge of Mazarin, his handsome person, graceful manners, and absolute devotion to her personal interests, untrammelled by French associations or sympathies, enchained her understanding and her heart.

Still the event of the struggle was long doubtful. It is evident from Mazarin's secret memoranda how great and how protracted were his fears and his uncertainty. When Madame de Chevreuse arrived in Paris she was received kindly, though somewhat coldly, by the Regent; the feudal party, still supported by the popular re-action, and numbering in its ranks the great majority of the clergy, nobility, and magistrates, and all Anne's favourite ladies, ranged itself under her banner. Had she played her cards with judgment, and consented to temporise in consideration of the difficulties of her mistress's position, she might, perhaps, have ultimately won the game. Old associations of friendship and service, the influence of religion, and the ties of family, the claims of gratitude and the dread of dishonour, were brought to bear, in all their force, on the Queen's mind by advocates to whose remonstrances, venerable character, or proved devotion gave almost irresistible weight. Anne would gladly have made considerable sacrifices in order to reconcile the rival factions and propitiate her old friends. She cheerfully abandoned to their hatred Chavigny, to whose counsels she attributed the last testament of her husband. Chavigny had been Mazarin's earliest friend and patron in France, and the two statesmen had continued up to this time bound to each other in close friendship; but the Cardinal connived without compunction at the disgrace of such a formidable competitor. He also, by the Queen's desire, made repeated overtures to Madame de Chevreuse for a union of interests, offering in return splendid advantages for herself and her friends. But the imperious Duchess, not deigning to inform herself of the real character of the Regent, or of the changes which time and circumstances had wrought during her six years of exile, spurned his advances, and insisted, as a preliminary act of justice, on the immediate restoration of Chateauneuf to the high office he had forfeited. Mazarin, however, had made up his mind to retire from France rather than accept such an able and unscrupulous colleague. And the Princess of Condé, whose wise counsels and tried friendship had just weight with the Regent, declared that the restoration of the late Keeper of the Seals to a leading post in the Government would alienate from it the support of her husband and son.

When Anne of Austria's positive refusal to recall Chateauneuf opened the eyes of the Importants to the altered state of her relations with them, their astonishment and fury knew no bounds. They overwhelmed her with the most bitter reproaches, with threats and insults. The Court rang with their angry complaints, not less distasteful to the Queen because in a measure well-founded, and

with obscene jests which made her blood boil.
She had become the political pupil of Mazarin,
and the private conferences which she held late
into every night with her handsome mentor, scandalised her friends, and furnished his opponents
with a fertile theme for scurrilous lampoons. The
insolent freedom and even rudeness of the Duke of
Beaufort, who on one occasion went so far as to
turn his back on her with a contemptuous gesture,
before the whole Court; the arrogant lectures of
the Duchess of Chevreuse; and the hostile attitude of the rest of the party gradually stifled her
natural feelings of compunction for the line of
policy she found it her interest to pursue.

Mazarin shaped his conduct with incomparable
art, and turned every circumstance to the best account. The quarrel between the Duchesses of
Longueville and Montbazon, breaking out at a
seasonable moment, linked the House of Condé
more firmly to his cause, and enabled him with
security to deal his adversaries a blow from
which they never recovered. Madame de Chevreuse and Beaufort, rendered desperate by defeat
and the exile of Madame de Montbazon, and unable to dislodge their wily antagonist by less
criminal means, contrived a plot for his assassination. The Cardinal, well served by his spies,
narrowly escaped with his life, and used the oppor-

tunity to bring matters to a crisis. Repairing to the Council of State, he demanded permission from the Regent to retire to Rome, unless she valued his services sufficiently to protect him from the malice of his enemies. He was warmly supported by the Prince of Condé, who detested the House of Vendôme. The Regent, now completely devoted to him, and weary of the insolence of the " Importants," agreed to sustain him by decisive measures. By her command, Beaufort was arrested at the Louvre, and shut up in the fortress of Vincennes. The Duke of Vendôme, Madame de Chevreuse, and, later on, even Madame de Hautefort, whose romantic loyalty and noble character adorn the pages of history and fiction, were banished from Court. The simple Bishop of Beauvais being no longer required to act as a screen to the favourite, was sent to his diocese. The most perilous services in the late reign, and the most humble submission to the new Government were not sufficient to atone for honest consistency and want of political foresight. The ingratitude of Anne of Austria was complete ; the policy of Richelieu triumphed, and Cardinal Mazarin took the helm as acknowledged Prime Minister.

CHAPTER IV.

THE first few years of Cardinal Mazarin's administration, if not unruffled by occasional storms, were on the whole sunny and tranquil. The impulse which the mighty genius of Richelieu had given to the State machine, carried it along smoothly for a long period after his death; and the milder policy of his successor rendered its pressure less galling. The nation, relieved from the iron grasp in which it had writhed for twenty years, breathed again with something of the rapture of recovered freedom. There was little open opposition. The Regent was gracious, profuse in her bounties, and popular. A witty courtier, commenting on the general satisfaction, declared that the French language was reduced to the five words, "The Queen is so good." The Minister was prudent and conciliating. The Court was splendid, and the arms of France were crowned with unprecedented glory. The vigour and decision with which the Importants had been quelled, caused the temporising state-craft of Mazarin to be ascribed to magnanimity and not to weakness.

Madame de Chevreuse alone of the Minister's foes stood forth in active opposition, undaunted and implacable. Banished to her country-house in Touraine, she resumed her treasonable correspondence with Spain, which in less fortunate days had been so zealously promoted by the Regent. But she soon found that she could not hope from the vigilant rancour of an ungrateful mistress, or the insensible heart of the Italian Cardinal, the partial indulgence she had so often experienced from Richelieu. A secret agent of the Government arrived at Tours to conduct her, as a state prisoner, to the Castle of Angouleme. The daring spirit which years before had borne her from the same spot, in the guise of a handsome young cavalier, in adventurous flight across the Pyrennees, animated her still; but the generous enemy who had supplied the funds for her romantic enterprise no longer existed. Penniless, but carrying concealed in her girdle the famous Cincini diamonds, she escaped from her house at night in disguise. Her daughter, a young girl of singular courage and beauty, was her only companion. The fugitives set out on foot for the coast of Brittany, braved extraordinary hardships, perils, and fatigues, and succeeded in reaching St. Malo.

The kindness of a Breton nobleman provided them with passages on board a ship bound for England; but the vessel was captured by an English man-of-war in the service of the Parliament, and the Duchess being recognised as a friend of Queen Henrietta Maria, was carried a prisoner to the Isle of Wight. It was proposed to deliver her up to the Regent. Fortunately for her, one of her old admirers, Lord Pembroke, was Governor of the Island, and he allowed her to depart for the Low Countries. The ill-starred wanderers reached Dunkirk in a lamentable plight, destitute of the commonest necessaries. The Duchess had only left her the mortifying resource of imploring the compassion of her old friend, the Archduke, from whom she had parted amidst such triumphal pomp, and with such magnificent promises, little more than a year before. Fallen and cheerless in themselves, and still sadder by contrast, were the fortunes of Madame de Chevreuse in her third exile from France. The political influence which formerly had made her an honoured guest at the greatest Courts of Europe, had in a large measure gone from her; and time and disappointment had dimmed the joyous sparkle of her wit, and the lustre of her radiant beauty. She took up her residence at Liege, pouring forth furious, but unheeded denunciations against Mazarin, or eating away her heart in sullen anger, until the return of troubled times restored her to her beloved Paris; to that life of reckless gaiety and restless intrigue which she loved so well.

Isolated cases of caballing like this of Madame de Chevreuse had, however, little effect on the general tranquillity of the kingdom. These were afterwards known as "the fair days of the Regency."

But the golden calm that glittered on the surface of events was delusive and transitory. Beneath it were at work all the elements of confusion; ill-defined, uncertain and oppressive authority; co-ordinate and conflicting claims and jurisdictions; the just resentments that spring from the constant violation of the rights of individual liberty and of property; the less just but more fierce resentments of depressed privilege, balked ambition, and exasperated pride; political and social corruption; and, underlying all, a vast writhing mass of helpless and hopeless misery. It was an age of transition. The whole mechanism of society was deranged. There was a want of harmony among the orders, a want of stability in the institutions of the State. The feudal system had been overthrown, but its ruins heaped everywhere in massive obstruction cumbered the land. The strong monarchical constitution which Richelieu had built up, he wanted leisure in his gigantic struggle with the House of Austria to consolidate and complete. The interests and pretensions he had crushed down began, as the memory of his rule grew fainter, to assert themselves again. Nor were these all of a character prejudicial to the State. Not only the selfish ambition of the great nobles, but also the ancient policy and patriotic aspirations of the Parliaments of the Kingdom, and more especially of the Parliament of Paris, aimed at confining the royal prerogative within straiter limits.

Until the 15th century the Kings of France had derived nearly the whole of their ordinary revenues from the royal domains. To supply the extraordinary expenses of Government, taxes were voted by the three Estates of the realm, and with one exception were levied in equitable proportions upon all classes. The exception was a direct tax called *" la taille,"* which fell exclusively on the Third Estate, the nobles being exemptedf rom it in consideration of the peculiar military obligations imposed upon them by the feudal system. Even the taille, however, could not be raised without the consent of the three Estates. Charles VII., by the assistance of the nobles, obtained from the nation, then smarting from the calamities that resulted from the English wars, the captivity of John, and the madness of Charles VI., the right of levying the taille by his own authority, in order to afford his people more effectual protection. As has been remarked by De Tocqueville, one of the ablest of modern French writers, this fatal concession was the origin of most of the political evils which have since afflicted France. In the beginning the taille amounted to no more than twelve hundred thousand livres, and was scarcely felt. But the French Kings soon increased it tenfold, and tacked on to it four other taxes, each of them as onerous as itself. The command of this large revenue enabled the Sovereign to maintain a standing army, which made him absolute ruler of the kingdom, and to dispense with the aid of the three Estates; the nobles conniving at innovations which increased their privileges and lightened their burdens, but prepared the way for universal servitude.

As the growing monarchy burst asunder its feudal trammels, the Convocation of the States-General came to be regarded as an extraordinary, and it generally proved an ineffective remedy for the perils or disorders of the kingdom; as a humiliating confession which every ruler shrank from, of scandalous misgovernment, or national calamity. In ordinary times the necessary work of legislation and finance was accomplished by means of Royal Edicts issued from the Council of State and registered in the first judicial court of the kingdom, the Parliament of Paris.

The proceeds of partial taxation soon proving insufficient to supply the ever-increasing expenditure of the Government, new resources were found in the creation and sale of innumerable public offices, which clogged every department of the administration. These offices, carrying with them special privileges, chiefly of immunity from the taille, were eagerly purchased by the rich inhabitants of the towns. The evils and the confusion produced by the multiplication of useless functionaries were enormous. Richelieu was said to have swept away one hundred thousand of these offices, but they soon sprang into existence again out of the necessities of the State. It was a favourite financial expedient of needy rulers arbitrarily to abolish posts which had been conferred for life, and almost immediately to re-establish in order to sell them again; the process being repeated until the strange avidity with which the French citizen sought after a place in the Administration was overpowered by the dread of confiscation. The Government also, whenever it was able, contracted loans at ruinous interest, which, however, was seldom paid. In fact, the Kings of France shrank from no means of procuring supplies, no matter how dishonourable or desperate, which might enable them to avoid calling together the Estates of their realm.

The increase of the King's prerogative was peculiarly oppressive to the commonalty. The clergy had their own assemblies, and their special privileges. To them and to the nobles, who were exempt from direct taxation, who had been relieved at the expense of the poorest class of the population from the equivalent obligations of military service imposed on them by the old feudal constitution, who monopolised public honours and employments, and possessed immunities which few sovereigns had either the wish or the power to infringe, the change was of little moment. But the Third Estate, which bore the weight of the public burthens, being deprived of the old constitutional means of representing their grievances and compelling redress, and being shut out from political life, found themselves without a voice in the State or a share in its prizes, exposed to the capricious tyranny of irresponsible power, and ground down by arbitrary exactions.

In this deplorable condition the Third Estate found occasional, though generally unsuccessful, champions, in the Parliaments or High Courts of Justice of the realm. There were eight of these great judicial bodies, the Parliament of Paris and seven provincial Parliaments; and with the inferior Courts they numbered forty thousand magistrates. The magisterial offices were acquired by purchase, conferred considerable dignity and emolument, especially in the capital, and were held for life. The Duke of Sully had, at the suggestion of a subordinate financier named Paulet, introduced a custom, by which the magistrates, in consideration of paying to the Crown an annual tax, called "le droit annuel" or "la Paulette," amounting to a sixtieth part of the original purchase-money, obtained the privilege of disposing of their posts, like other property, by will, or in case of intestacy, of securing the reversion of them to their natural heirs. This privilege was granted for periods of nine years, renewable at the pleasure of the King; and, though the termination of a period might sometimes furnish occasion for an extraordinary demand upon the purses of the magistrates, no desire had been shown by any minister to extinguish a custom which, if strange, worked well, because it was in harmony with the genius of the people. It was not uncommon to find members of the same family holding magisterial appointments for several succeeding generations. In this manner was formed a nobility of the robe, sprung from the bourgeois class, of high legal training and culture, renowned for its independence and integrity, possessing considerable influence, not only on account of its elevated character and functions, but also of its popular sympathies, and illustrating the annals of France by many splendid examples of learning, courage, and virtue.

The Parliament of Paris held pre-eminence among the judicial bodies of the kingdom. It was the final Court of Appeal and the King's own Court, where he held Beds of Justice and caused his edicts to be registered. It counted among its members the Princes of the Blood and the peers of the realm, and had jurisdiction over them. In the Palace of Justice it possessed an august temple worthy of its venerable dignity. Around it, in the same spacious edifice, clustered four inferior Courts, of Inquests, Requests, Aids, and Accounts, which, on occasions of great public or professional interest, its First President was accustomed to convoke for the purpose of general deliberation. In troubled periods, when the Executive was weak, and particularly during a Royal minority, it frequently asserted its freedom, and refused to give by registration the force of laws to oppressive or unpopular mandates of the Crown. It claimed the right of freely discussing the edicts it was called upon to register, and of rejecting those it disapproved. But, in the eyes of the Sovereign, it was the duty of Parliament to register all his edicts, and its liberty of dissent was limited to a barren right of remonstrance, which he was always free to disregard. He was accustomed to repress its opposition by holding a Bed of Justice and causing the obnoxious decree to be entered upon the journals in his presence; by imprisoning refractory members; and even by banishing the whole body to some provincial town. Richelieu, in order to annihilate its pretensions, compelled the Parliament of Paris to register a decree declaring its own incompetency to meddle with affairs of State. But on the death of Louis XIII., the Regent, seeking support from all quarters, had revived the ambitious hopes of the members of the High Court by submitting, contrary to Mazarin's advice, her husband's political testament to their judgment, by accepting unrestricted authority from their hands, and by promising to be guided on all occasions by their counsels. The Parliament of Paris indeed claimed to be, by ancient usage, the guardian of the Sovereign during his minority; and its members, though animated by patriotic sentiments and full of zeal for the interests of their order, were generally governed by a spirit of wise moderation, and of deep reverence for the Royal authority. But the inferior Courts, to the offices of which less responsibility and less consideration attached, contained many magistrates of more turbulent and ambitious temper, who were strongly stirred by the awakening of popular freedom in a neighbouring country. The bold spirit of inquiry and innovation which found voice in the subordinate chambers, insensibly stimulated the views of the higher magistrates. Encouraged not only by its relations with the Regent, and the internal situation of France, but also in some degree by the example of resistance to tyrannical power which England was at that time exhibiting, the Parliament of Paris was not indisposed to seize a favourable occasion of restraining the abuses of the prerogative, and at the same time of vindicating and augmenting its own political importance.

The discontent of the great nobles of the feudal party and their numerous adherents among the lesser nobility was a pregnant source of danger, not only to the tranquillity, but to the welfare of the kingdom, because they were actuated mainly by sordid motives, and acknowledged in their public conduct no principle of patriotism or justice. An unusual combination of circumstances, skilfully turned to account by the arts of Mazarin, rendered them unable during many years to arise from the political quagmire into which they had been precipitated by their own folly and the vigour of the Regent. The policy of Richelieu had destroyed much of their ancient power. Their proceedings at the commencement of the Regency had discredited them in the eyes of the nation. For the first time during a long period in the history of France they were totally bereft of the support of the Princes of the Blood. Their old chief, the Duke of Orleans, now Lieutenant-General of the realm, but with little real authority or influence, was absolutely ruled by his favourite the Abbé la Riviere, whose services Mazarin had purchased by the promise of a Cardinal's hat. With La Riviere's assistance, Monsieur was alternately terrified and cajoled by the Regent into a docile acquiescence in all her measures. The House of Condé, gorged with offices and radiant with glory, steadily supported a system which gratified all its wishes. The princes of Vendôme, banished or imprisoned, sought by abject submission and by a family alliance with the all-powerful minister, to recover the advantages they had lost. Stripped of their dignities, cast off by the Regent, forsaken by their natural leaders, and depressed by a long series of disasters, the party of the old nobility were reduced to a state of passive dissatisfaction.

Mazarin had weakened them still further by playing upon the selfish aspirations of their leading members in separate negotiations, and by keeping alive the hopes of all with occasional favours, and unbounded promises. But the multitude of claims far exceeded his inclination or his power to concede; and the discontent of the feudal party, though impotent for the present, was the more dangerous because sustained by brilliant talents and courage, and leavened by extraordinary political and social profligacy.

The century of faction and civil war which followed the death of Henry II. completely demoralised the upper classes of French society. It killed patriotism and public spirit; and generated a condition of political turpitude for which a parallel can scarcely be found in any other country or period of modern history. Its effect on private morality was equally disastrous. Scoffing impiety, which held nothing sacred among the living or among the dead, which profaned with impartial ribaldry the mysteries of the altar and the tomb; coarse debauchery, which ostentatiously violated the decencies of life; assassination by open violence and secret poisoning, were frightfully prevalent. The trade of the poisoner was associated with traffic in spells, and the detestable charlatanism of sorcery; blasphemous unbelief, and diabolical superstition going hand-in-hand. Duelling, which Richelieu had sternly repressed, grew after his death into wholesale butchery. Chastity excited so much contempt, that women of strict virtue affected vice, in order to escape disagreeable criticism. The most brilliant epochs of French history have been generally characterised by sensuality, in which the magic garb of graceful refinement softened what was repulsive, and heightened every charm. The period of which we are treating was illustrated not only by the glory of arms, but by unsurpassed intellectual activity; but notwithstanding the decorum that reigned in her own household, the licentiousness of the Court of Anne of Austria was grossness itself. The noble examples of virtue that adorned the age only deepened the contrast presented by the general corruption. At a time of avowed scepticism pervading every sphere and every relation of life, of contempt of all laws, human and divine, there were many of both sexes, in positions most exposed to the contagion, who were governed by a spirit of faith, of noble self-sacrifice, and of chivalrous fidelity worthy of the ages of the Crusaders. It was the time of St. Vincent de Paul, who most of all men brought divine charity to hallow, and console human misery; and nowhere did the words and works of the venerable teacher fall upon a more fruitful soil than in the fashionable world of Paris. It was the time of the "divine Arthenice," and her circle of the Hotel Rambouillet, which for purity of tone, not less than splendid versatility of genius and all the charms of refined society, is without a rival in ancient or modern civilization. But it was still more the time of the poet Scarron and of Ninon de l'Enclos, whose saloons were temples of fashion, where wit and beauty, genius and Christian virtue itself, were prostituted in the service of atheism and obscenity.

Perhaps the most extraordinary sign and effect of the deterioration of manners was the easy toleration practised on points regarding which women, at least, are usually most sensitive; the throwing down of the social barriers which ordinarily separate women of good and of evil repute. The affectionate wife of the godless and debauched, though not ungenerous buffoon, the intimate companion of the shameless courtezan, was a young lady of spotless reputation, whom piety and strict principles, even more than her undoubted beauty and accomplishments, afterwards raised, under the name of Madame de Maintenon, to the most splendid throne of the world. Bussy Rabutin, who used his rare wit to season disgusting licentiousness and outrageous impiety, was the cherished correspondent of Madame de Sevigné. Mademoiselle de Hautefort, whose whole life was sublime in its self-sacrificing virtue, was the bosom friend of Madame de Chevreuse. When the distinctions which women of unblemished character are accustomed to preserve with the greatest tenacity were so utterly confounded, it was not to be expected that their frail sisters should, in their conduct, pay morality the homage of outward decorum. An amusing instance of this absence of restraint, even in the highest circles of Parisian life, may serve as an illustration of the prevalent tone of morals. The co-adjutor Archbishop of Paris, the celebrated Paul Gondi, afterwards Cardinal de Retz, neither whose remarkable ugliness nor sacred profession prevented his acquiring a dubious *éclat* for conquests over the fair, had been for some time notoriously the lover of the Princess of Gueminée. Unhappily for the lady's repose, Mademoiselle de Chevreuse, a younger, more captivating, and equally frail beauty, seduced the heart of the inconstant prelate. The fickleness of a gay Archbishop was not a circumstance so uncommon at the time as to provoke more than passing comment; and had the Princess dissembled her chagrin, and quietly consoled herself by taking another lover, or by making the most of those that remained to her,

her disappointment would have been speedily forgotten. But the perfidy of the coadjutor appears to have converted the dove-like tenderness of Madame de Gueminée into all the rage of the vulture. Meeting him soon after his desertion of her in a fashionable saloon, in a transport of jealous anger she flung a foot-stool at his head, to the intense amusement of a brilliant assemblage of his flock, who had the happiness to witness the scene.

Debauched, factious, rapacious, and impoverished, without principle and without fear, the feudal party only awaited an opportunity and a leader to plunge the realm into confusion in the hope of turning the public misfortunes to their own advantage.

Such an occasion as they sought could hardly fail to arise sooner or later from the well-founded and increasing discontent of the middle and lower classes, and from the inevitable mistakes which the Regent and Mazarin, both foreigners, both imperfectly acquainted with the institutions and character of the people they ruled, would commit with greater frequency and more fatal results, as their course became obscured by gathering troubles. The bourgeois and the peasants, whose industry fed a war of unprecedented severity and costliness, and the pomp of an extravagant Court, were crushed beneath a weight of arbitrary taxation, which became more intolerable every day. France had for many years maintained four or five separate armies in the field, besides paying large subsidies to Sweden; and still the stubborn spirit of the House of Austria was unsubdued. Agriculture languished everywhere from the incessant drain upon the flower of the male population; large districts were waste and depopulated; manufactures and trade were slowly perishing under exorbitant imposts; and the commonalty execrated a war equally opposed to their national interests and their religious sympathies. The misery of the peasants was aggravated by the cruel rapacity of the Royal Intendents and the wealthy financiers, who farmed the public revenues and fattened on the general ruin. As Omer Talon, the eloquent Attorney General in the Parliament of Paris, said, in representing their condition to the Queen, "They only possessed their souls because a soul could not be sold by auction." Their groans and prayers, though loud and piteous, were listened to in silence. But though the cries of the helpless and famished people might be treated with indifference, the jealous policy which had led Mazarin to exclude from a share in the government the most able and experienced of the statesmen who had been formed by Richelieu, gradually involved him in troubles, and raised up against him antagonisms which it was impossible for him to disregard.

On the dismissal of Chavigny and his father, Bouthillier, from their offices of Secretary of State, in the early days of the Regency, the Cardinal had filled the vacant places with two creatures of his own—Le Tellier, a Frenchman, a diligent and submissive subordinate, became Secretary for Foreign Relations, and Particelli, a Siamese adventurer, better known by his French title of the Chevalier d'Eméry, was placed over the finances. Few historical characters have been sketched by more skilful hands, few have come down to us pourtrayed in darker colours than the Chevalier d'Eméry. Able, courageous, and witty, but luxurious, dissolute, rapacious, cruel, faithless, and cynical, he made a jest of all moral obligations, and with reckless scorn openly mocked at the miseries aggravated by his corrupt administration. The proceeds of the existing taxes, however burdensome, were insufficient to satisfy the calls upon the royal exchequer. Instead of rendering these taxes more productive by removing the frightful abuses of collection, which impoverished at once the Treasury and the people, Eméry only thought of confusing inextricably the public accounts in order to hide his own peculations, and perhaps those of Mazarin. As it was impossible to wring further supplies from the ruined peasants, he applied his mind to the discovery of some new process of extortion which might be brought to bear on the wealthy citizens of Paris. Searching among the ancient statutes of the realm, he disinterred from the dust of ages obsolete enactments, the revival of which promised to accomplish his ends. One, passed about a hundred years before, in the reign of Henry II., to prevent the extension of the city of Paris, and long fallen into disuse, placed whole quarters of the capital at the disposal of the Crown. Eméry took immediate steps to put it into execution. The inhabitants of some of the most wealthy regions of Paris received orders to demolish their houses, or to redeem them by payment of enormous fines. The rage and consternation of the Parisians knew no bounds. They appealed for protection to the Parliament, and this body remonstrated with the Regent against the act of confiscation contemplated by her ministers. Anne of Austria, unmindful of her repeated professions of deference to the advice of the magistrates, and of the cautious councils of Mazarin, repelled this interference with a haughty scorn which would have appeared harsh in Richelieu himself. But the tumults that shook the capital scared the Cardinal.

In conjunction with the patriotic Chief President of the High Court, he prevailed on the Regent to assent to a compromise. The obnoxious edict was withdrawn, and the Municipal Council of Paris voted a subsidy to replenish the exchequer.

This extraordinary supply, however, only enabled the Government to tide over the financial difficulties of the current year. The charges of the war, the profuse magnificence of the Court, the corruption of the administration, underwent no diminution as the exhaustion of the country increased; and Eméry, in order to meet the growing deficiencies of the revenue, again and again brought forward measures for the purpose of extracting money from the rich inhabitants of the capital. He still continued to take from the wellstored armoury of finance, which his researches had discovered, the rusted weapons of past legislation, because by reviving imposts which at some time had received the sanction of the Parliament of Paris, which, though dormant, had never been repealed, he hoped to avoid the opposition which might attend demands for the registration of new fiscal enactments. Some of his expedients, such as a forced grant from the notables of Paris, were simply extortion. Others, as the imposition of octroi duties, were in themselves defensible. But all were harshly and arbitrarily enforced, and all were resisted with animosity, which deepened and widened every day.

At the beginning of these disputes one or other of the inferior courts of justice was most frequently the organ of the popular discontent, the High Court of Parliament giving a general support to the authority of the Regent. The office of First President of the High Court, an office pre-eminent in dignity and authority in the French judicial system, was at this time filled by perhaps the greatest magistrate that even Monarchical France, which ranked an unrivalled line of illustrious magistrates among its chief glories, ever produced. This was Mathieu Molé, a man of high wisdom, spotless integrity, unexampled courage, and iron will; a profound jurist, a master of grave, earnest eloquence, and of polished irony; moderate in his views, a firm supporter of the throne and the laws, and an enlightened advocate of popular rights. Molé—Conservative by habit of mind, and the jealous guardian of the privileges of his court, which the impatient spirits who had sway in the subordinate courts showed a disposition to invade—for some time firmly resisted the pressure, and repressed the pretensions of the inferior chambers. If the Regent had been wise, she would perhaps have found safety for her government in the dissensions of the magistracy. But,

incensed at the license of speech permitted in the
Court of Inquests, she arrested some of its presidents and councillors, and flung them into prison.
This despotic proceeding aroused against her the
esprit de corps, which was perhaps the strongest
sentiment among the French magistrates. The
companies, united by common danger, forgot their
disputes. Convoked by Molé, they unanimously
protested against the Queen's arbitrary act, and
demanded the release or trial of the prisoners.
The haughty disdain and the fierce menaces with
which the Regent repelled what she termed their
presumption, only heightened their irritation.
The state of the kingdom and the progress of
events daily furnished them with new motives for
strict union. The infancy of the King, the abasement of the feudal party and absence of its leading members, the abuse of the royal authority by
the foreigners, who monopolised its functions, the
spreading spirit of resistance, seemed to invite the
Parliament of Paris to assume the position it had
long coveted, that of constitutional organ of the
national wants and wishes, controlling the legislative and financial powers of the Crown.

This aim had no positive sanction, though it
might find some colourable pretexts, in the ancient
usages of the realm. The Parliament was a
judicial body, and the political functions which it

sought to exercise belonged of right to the States-General. But the States had not assembled since the early part of the century, and they met only at the pleasure of the Crown. The old feudal checks on the prerogative had been swept away. The High Court was distinguished above all existing public bodies in the kingdom by ancient dignity, disciplined vigour, legislative and judicial authority, and a higher and wider representative character. The disorders of the realm, and the confidence and veneration of the people, lent the motives and character of patriotism to its secret ambition. Baser motives, it is true—love of intrigue, self-interest, and private rancour—were at work among its members, as well as among the members of the subordinate courts. Disappointed politicians, who had no sympathy with its aims, secretly stimulated its action. Chavigny, Chateauneuf, and the Coadjutor De Retz, three men of first-rate ability, each of whom was equal to the greatest employments, and all of whom were jealously excluded by Mazarin from the administration, possessed numerous adherents in the Chambers, and silently promoted opposition to the Government for the purpose of overthrowing the Prime Minister. The Coadjutor especially exercised a large and an increasing influence amongst the younger and more factious members. But the majority of the High Court and the most respected magistrates steadily followed the lead of their First President, who, even when reluctantly lending his sanction to perilous and irregular steps, was swayed by a paramount sense of public duty; whose upright and steadfast mind was equally proof against seductions of popular applause or the terrors of popular fury, and the violence or blandishments of the Court.

The dangers that threatened the Government from the opposition of the Parliament of Paris, trifling at first, but more menacing every year, were greatly aggravated by the deficiencies and the errors of Cardinal Mazarin. The business of foreign relations, which he retained under his own immediate control, and for which he possessed unrivalled qualifications, was conducted with admirable skill and vigour. But his consciousness of the peculiar difficulties of his position as Prime Minister, working upon a temper not naturally bold, rendered the internal policy of the Government feeble and undignified. His knowledge of the laws, the customs, the institutions, and even the language of the kingdom, was at this time extremely imperfect. He had no stand-point in the State except the favour of the Regent. His love of power had deprived him of the assistance of any French statesman on whose capacity, experience, and sincerity he could rest with confidence. Like a blind man groping along a strange and difficult path, a perpetual fear of incurring some unknown peril infected his mind with a fatal irresolution as to the steps he should pursue. Haunted by chimerical terrors, he was in a great measure unaware of the real dangers that encompassed him. His favourite political maxim, that selfishness in its narrowest sense is the universal motive of human actions, was a feeble safe-guard against the rising passions of a stormy age. And in his partiality for finesse, he could not even allow this cardinal principle of his system free play. Reluctant to part with a talisman to which he ascribed such potent influence, he kept an object of desire dangling before the eyes of some opponent whom he purposed to conciliate until, at length, disappointment produced incurable irritation. His policy was to avoid present dangers and to pave the way for the action of his trusted ally, Time, by cautious steering and temporising expedients.

The haughty Austrian blood of the Regent suggested to her a very different line of proceeding. She remembered in what abject submission the Parliament of Paris had cowered before Richelieu; how it had seen Mary of Medicis, the Princes of the Blood, and the greatest nobles of the realm, imprisoned, exiled, condemned to death by irregular special commissions, without daring to utter a protest. And she took no pains to conceal her anger and contempt at the presumption which now assailed the throne with remonstrances on behalf of a few turbulent councillors, mere pitiful *canaille*. Had she followed the promptings of her own judgment while the imperious spirit of the late Cardinal still informed the administration and awed the realm, she might probably have crushed opposition in the bud. But she constantly allowed herself to be swayed from her convictions of the necessity of ruling with a strong hand by the timorous counsels of her minister. The result was a halting and uncertain policy, the most dangerous of any. The scornful words and the violent acts of the Queen, explained away in sugared phrases by the Cardinal, and followed by ungracious concessions, encouraged and inflamed the opposition of the magistrates and the citizens, and exposed the Government to contempt.

The animosity with which the Parisians regarded him was intensified by singular want of foresight on the part of Mazarin, who, laying aside, as his position became more secure, the prudence that had governed the beginning of his career, insulted the public distress by displaying in magnificent buildings, and in ostentatious luxury, the enormous wealth he had already amassed. At the time of the downfall of the Importants, Anne of Austria, anxious to escape from the sad memories and the discomforts of the Louvre, had removed her Court to the splendid and spacious palace which Richelieu had built and had bequeathed to his sovereign. The recent attempt on his life, and her constant need of his guidance in affairs of State, did not perhaps permit her to see in its full extent the imprudence she committed in assigning her favourite a suite of apartments adjoining her own. The Cardinal, safely installed in the Palais Royal, and with uncontrolled command of the public revenue, indulged without restraint his sumptuous and refined tastes. The most renowned artists of Italy, architects, painters, musicians, were invited to embellish and delight the French capital. The art collections of his native land, an almost inexhaustible and as yet unspoiled treasury of genius, were ransacked to satisfy the luxurious wants of a minister, who united faultless judgment to boundless resources. Statues, pictures, cabinets, vases, the most sublime and exquisite achievements of Italian masters, arriving day after day at the Palais Royal, excited the wonder and envy of the Parisians. Contiguous to, and as if in rivalry of Richelieu's noble pile, there soon arose, under the skilful hand of the great French architect, Mansard, from the midst of vast and beautiful gardens, a fitting home for so many artistic gems; the superb proportions of the Palais Mazarin, rich externally in various hues of sculptured marble, and decorated within by the brilliant pencils of the greatest painters of the time. The prodigious sums squandered in operatic entertainments, hitherto unknown in France, to which the Cardinal invited the Court, excited loud murmurs of public indignation. The unwise ostentation which paraded before all eyes the colossal private fortune that grew apace with the beggary of the Treasury, the wretchedness of the people, and the needs of the State, was sure to provoke the Nemesis that waits upon insolent prosperity. Three young damsels, the first migration of the celebrated nieces of Mazarin, arriving from Rome in the middle of 1647, to be educated under the care of Anne of Austria, afforded new point to the furious tirades of the Parisians. Rhyming lampoons—of which the Mazarinades by the Abbé Scarron were the most famous—witty, obscene, audacious, and truculent, in which the Regent, Mazarin, and the Mazarinettes, aspersed with the grossest license, were held up to public hatred and contempt, began to be chaunted in the streets and under the windows of the palace. The placable and subtle

Cardinal, with his tortuous policy and his gentle expedients, found that, without avoiding the fierce enmities that had been aroused by the vigorous despotism of his predecessor, he had made himself the object of popular scorn.

It was in this unfavourable state of public opinion that the Government felt itself compelled by the exigences of its position to send for registration to the Parliament of Paris new financial decrees, necessary in order to provide for the expenditure of the year 1648. Every year the task of Eméry had become more difficult and more odious. The methods in which he could exercise his perverted ingenuity diminished through an inevitable process of exhaustion, as the public exasperation grew more vehement. But it seemed to the Queen and Mazarin, that the peculiar constitution of the French Magistracy now gave them a fortunate advantage over the Parliament, which afforded effectual means at once of repression and of extortion. The period of nine years, during which the Magistrates, through the payment of the Paulette, possessed an absolute property in their offices, expired with the year 1647. The renewal of the lease, though rendered almost a matter of form by the custom of fifty years, was an act of the Sovereign's favour. The Government preserved an ominous silence on the subject. As an additional safeguard against the dreaded opposition of the High Court, it was determined that the financial edicts should be secretly prepared in the Council of State, and presented for registration in a Bed of Justice.

The holding of a Bed of Justice for the purpose of suppressing unwelcome discussion was the most odious and absolute exercise of the royal prerogative. The King went in state to the Palace of Justice, and peremptorily ordered his edict, of which only the title was read out, to be entered on the journals in his presence. The theory on which this arbitrary stretch of authority rested, was that the wisdom and piety inherent in Kings of France shaped even their most apparently unjust decisions, by suggesting to them motives of high and beneficent policy inscrutable to less gifted mortals. But the special attribute of divinely enlightened judgment in the affairs of State, with whatever colour of probability it might be credited to a Saint Louis, or even to an ordinary monarch of mature understanding, could hardly be seriously predicated by the most devoted loyalty of a child of nine years. The boy-king performed his part, and departed amidst the respectful silence of the Parliament. When it was found that the new edicts, besides other measures of spoliation, created twelve additional offices of Masters of Requests, exposed for sale in the ordinary way, and greatly diminishing the value of those already existing, the uproar in the Court of Requests was loud and angry. An intimation from the Government that the privilege of the Paulette would be granted to the members of the inferior Chambers, the exception in favour of the High Court being one of Mazarin's over-subtle strokes of finesse, only on the payment of four years' income of their appointments into the Exchequer, rendered the tumult general. The Parliament, true to its order, refused to separate its interests from those of the other Courts, and in defiance of the Regent's menaces, annulled the objectionable clauses of the Royal edict. Anne of Austria, furious at this unprecedented contempt of the Sovereign's own act, retracted her concessions in regard to the Paulette, arrested several of the more obnoxious Councillors, and threatened the High Court with summary vengeance. But private wrongs acted as a powerful incentive to patriotic zeal. The Parliament, undaunted, threw down the gauge of battle by passing the celebrated Decree of Union of the 13th of May, 1648, which convoked all the Chambers in the Hall of St. Louis to deliberate for the reformation of the realm.

This bold measure struck the Cardinal with dismay. By his instructions, the Chancellor

Seguier sent a conciliatory message to the Palace
of Justice. "Tell the Chancellor," replied Molé,
"that we shall no longer permit our private
interests to remain at the mercy of a Controller
General, or trust the administration of the realm
to a foreigner." The Regent was now beside herself with amazement and anger. The cautious
counsels of her minister began, too late, to fill her
with distrust. She flung four more of the magistrates into the Bastille; and she sent Guinégaud,
Under Secretary of State, to the Palace of Justice
with an order in Council cancelling the Decree of
Union, and directing that it should be torn in his
presence from the Parliamentary Register and
replaced by the decree of cassation. Guinégaud,
arriving with an armed escort, was received by
the excited magistrates with a running fire of
taunts and revilings, and compelled to retreat
in confusion without having accomplished his
mission. Then the Regent, incensed to the last
degree, commanded Molé and his colleagues to
appear on the morrow at the Palais Royal and
deliver up the leaf of their Register containing the
obnoxious decree. The Parliament, after a sharp
debate, resolved to obey the Queen's summons to
the Palace; but their decision on the question
of surrendering the coveted leaf was expressed
in the energetic words of the First President,

"*Nec possumus, nec debemus.*" On the following day the Regent, with the young King by her side, surrounded by the great officers of the Crown, and by an unusual parade of military force, ascended her throne in the State apartments of the Palais Royal to receive the submission of the Parliament. The courtiers, not doubting the result, exulted with quiet malice over the approaching spectacle of humiliation. But when Molé, conspicuous by his magnificent head and his long white beard, announced the decision of the Chamber, this serene placidity was torn by conflicting emotions. The most violent counsels were discussed, but the prudent advice of Mazarin, which found a secret echo in the hearts of many of the loudest declaimers, prevailed. The magistrates were warned of the chastisement they would incur by further contumacy in a solemn lecture from the Chancellor, which the Queen greatly enlivened by fitful explosions of uncontrollable passion, and were then permitted to depart in safety. They proceeded without delay to carry out the Decree of Union by holding the first meeting of all the Chambers in the Hall of St. Louis.

It is necessary to bear in mind the principles and the characters of the Regent and Cardinal Mazarin in order to appreciate the disturbed, yet dissimilar feelings with which they received the news of this deliberate act of defiance. Both of them were unable to understand the meaning of popular rights. In the eyes of both absolute monarchy was the only just and legitimate form of Government, and opposition in any shape, or upon any pretext, was rebellion. But the mind of Anne of Austria, incapable of fear, and filled with contempt for the plebeian magistrates, was occupied only with thoughts of vengeance; while the Cardinal was only too keenly alive to the perils of the situation. "God grant me patience," Anne would exclaim; "the Cardinal is too easy; he will ruin everything by always sparing and propitiating his enemies." "You, madame," Mazarin would retort, "are like a young recruit; you fight, but you know not your danger." In fact, the Parliament occupied a position of great advantage. They were strong in the cordial sympathy of the provincial parliaments, in the universal discontent, and in the enthusiastic support of Paris. The great nobles alienated from the Government beheld its difficulties with satisfaction. Orleans, feeble and fond of popularity, could not be relied on. In Condé, in whom Anne of Austria recognised a spirit congenial to her own, lay, notwithstanding his continual bickerings with Mazarin, her chief dependence. But the Prince, with ill-appointed and mutinous troops, had his hands full on the Flemish frontier. The taxes for the year could not be levied. The treasury was empty. Large arrears of pay were due to the armies and to the officers of the Court. The Queen had to pledge her jewels and to borrow money from the Dowager Princess of Condé, in order to defray the current expenses of her household, and to pay the Royal Guards, the only military force she could oppose to an outbreak of the capital.

Turning, in her distress, to a minister who had administered with ability the arbitrary system of Richelieu, and fallen from power through his perfidy for her, which she had fitly repaid by ingratitude, the Regent summoned Chateauneuf from his retreat at Montrouge, and asked his assistance. But the wily old ex-keeper, finding that he was expected to take the chestnuts out of the fire for Mazarin, declined the responsibility, and counselled concessions. She then secretly invited Condé to Paris to save the Crown. The Prince, who had left his army in presence of the superior force of the Archduke Leopold, could only advise her to temporise until the conclusion of the campaign. Sick at heart, and having no further resource, she accepted the Decree of Union.

The committee appointed by the United Chambers, of which Molé was chairman, distrusting the Regent's sincerity, lost no time in framing and submitting for her sanction a constitution of twenty-seven articles. One article abolished the office of Royal Intendant, and diminished the impost called " la taille," which pressed so heavily on the peasants. A second prohibited, under penalty of death, the levying of new taxes, except such as might be imposed by edicts registered after full discussion and free consent, by the Parliament of Paris. A third article restrained the Crown from creating new judicial or financial offices without the consent of the Parliament. By a fourth it was provided that no Frenchman should remain in prison longer than twenty-four hours without being taken before his legal judges—a provision equivalent to the Habeas Corpus Act, passed at a later period in England. These were the more important points of this famous constitution. It will be seen that it not only swept away a financial system, fertile in fraud, oppression, and injustice, but that it lopped away the most monstrous abuses of the royal prerogative; the power of compelling decrees to be registered without examination in Beds of Justice, and the power of arbitrarily arresting any subject, however blameless, and detaining him in prison during the King's pleasure.

The reforms embodied in the new constitution were resisted by the Government with the greatest pertinacity. The suppression of the Royal Intendants touched it, to borrow the words of the Coadjutor De Retz, "in the very apple of the eye." These functionaries, who farmed the collection of the taxes, covenanted to pay a fixed sum into the Treasury, and wrung immense profits from the famine-stricken people. They were in the habit of advancing the stipulated amount at the beginning of each year. The Government was already indebted to them for large loans which it had nott he means of repaying, and was in the direst need of additional advances. But the magistrates were not to be moved by argument or expostulation, and the Intendants fell. Mazarin, by an unworthy breach of faith, accepted with alacrity the proposal of the incensed Parliament to relieve the State by cancelling its liabilities to the discarded financiers, who were branded as public robbers. In order further to appease popular hatred, Eméry was dismissed from the post of Controller General, and exiled from Paris.

The Regent also, after long demur, and in a manner that left no doubt of the insincerity of the concession, partially allowed the articles upon taxation, and freedom of discussion and suffrage. But it was impossible to obtain her assent to the provision against arbitrary imprisonment. She declared she was ready to brave every peril rather than suffer the prerogative to be robbed of its brightest jewel. In violation of her recent pledges, she again brought the young King to the Palace of Justice to command the registration of the accepted articles in a mutilated form, which destroyed their efficacy; and to prohibit the further meetings of the United Chambers in the Hall of St. Louis. At the same time, with the view of rendering this arbitrary proceeding palatable, the privileges of the Paulette were renewed unconditionally for another period. But the Parliament, justly indignant, treated the royal edict with contempt; and matters would have come to a crisis had not the Duke of Orleans, whose gracious manners and popular bearing during the late discussions, in which he frequently represented the Crown, won him universal favour, been induced by Mazarin to implore a short adjournment of the political debates in the Hall of St. Louis, as a mark of regard towards himself.

It was perfectly clear, however, to both sides that no compromise was possible. Only a decisive victory could end the conflict. The Regent regarding the unexpected assault of the Parliament upon the undoubted, though tyrannical prerogatives of the Crown as flagrant treason, and naturally resenting the advantage it had taken of the embarrasments of the Government in order to usurp a character and powers foreign to its constitution and its functions, eagerly expected an opportunity of striking a blow which might vindicate the royal authority and quell for ever such insolent pretensions. On the other hand, Molé and his colleagues, moved by patriotic indignation at seeing the public miseries aggravated by the misrule of foreign adventurers, were determined to destroy for ever the abuses of authority that scourged the country; to pursue their present advantage to the utmost, in order to wring from the Regent a full and formal concession of all their demands. And it must be admitted that their proceedings, though irregular, were fully justified by the circumstances of the time. The fall of the great feudal houses had removed the chief restraint upon the authority of the King. It was no longer in the power of any one order of the State to compel the Sovereign to call together the States General; and a union of the orders for that purpose, separated as the nobles and the higher clergy were from the Third Estate, by peculiar privileges and interests, and by the contempt of dominant race, could only be brought about by some overwhelming crisis of public affairs. The superior dignity and consideration it enjoyed in the State, the impartial position it held as the chief guardian and exponent of the laws, its ancient traditions as the courageous defender of the rights of the subject, the crying evils of misgovernment, and, above all, the loud call of public opinion, had imposed on the Parliament the lofty and perilous duty of finding a remedy for the disorders of the kingdom. Guided hitherto by a few wise, resolute, and high-principled statesmen, the propositions of reform it had submitted were equitable and moderate, laying the foundations of secure and well-ordered freedom, without unnecessarily trenching on the power and dignity of the Crown. The Parliamentary leaders saw that Anne of Austria and her minister were not to be trusted. They discerned, too, with patriotic insight, what the astute Cardinal and his imperious mistress could not see in their imperfect acquaintance with the real condition of France, and perhaps would not see if they could, that the political atmosphere was full of the signs and portents of an approaching convulsion. The country had gradually drifted into that unhappy condition in which change appears to all classes to mean improvement. The nobles ardently desired a state of confusion which would promote their own selfish aims. The bourgeois class, incensed by misgovernment, and stirred by the sound of the revolutionary tempest that had swept over England, were ripe for revolt. The peasantry having tasted the bitterest dregs of misery had nothing further to fear. Only prompt and ample concessions on the part of the Crown could now avert from the kingdom the calamities of civil war.

It is at such periods of general discontent that men of bold, unscrupulous genius appear prominently on the political stage, and, rousing the passions of a nation into tumult, are borne to greatness on the mighty wave of popular opinion. There was not now wanting a man of this stamp in France, one of the most skilful and accomplished artificers of faction that the world had ever seen; a powerful but sombre spirit, whose delight it was to ride on the whirlwind and play with the lightnings of political convulsion, to rule in fierce triumph the wild forces of anarchy; who, to serve his own ambition, collecting all the heterogeneous and discordant elements of disaffection in France, marshalled them against the Government in uncongenial association under the celebrated name of the Fronde. This was Paul Gondi, afterwards Archbishop of Paris and Cardinal de Retz. Gondi was born of the ducal house of De Retz, which derived its origin from a Florentine banker, who had come to France in the train of Catherine of Medicis, and whose family had been enriched and raised to the highest rank of French nobility by the partial favour of Charles IX. Nature had formed him for the profession of arms; but, being a younger son, family interests compelled him to enter the Church. During the latter part of Richelieu's life, the little Abbé de Retz became notorious for his amours, his duels, and his active participation in plots for the assassination or overthrow of the minister. The Cardinal, although he seems to have regarded the turbulent priest with a feeling of misgiving similar to that which had sharpened Sulla's aversion for Julius Cæsar, to whose early character and career those of De Retz bore a striking resemblance, dealt leniently with him; and, after the death of Louis XIII., to whom he was odious, the young Abbé was appointed by Anne of Austria Coadjutor to his uncle, the Archbishop of Paris. This dignity, which secured to him the reversion of the Metropolitan See, and gave him a recognised position in the State, was only the first step in the ladder of his ambition. He aspired to tread in the footsteps of Richelieu —to become Cardinal and Prime Minister of France. Pursuing this object, he assiduously cultivated the favour of the Regent, and sought to fling over her the dangerous spells of his lively wit and his brilliant fancy, until Mazarin, discerning a dangerous rival, frustrated his schemes by skilfully throwing an air of ridicule around the pretensions of the gay but ill-favoured prelate. He then changed his tactics. Seeing clearly that Mazarin's hold upon the mind and heart of Anne of Austria was not to be shaken, and that his own way to greatness lay over the ruined fortunes of the subtle Italian, he set himself to raise such troubles in the kingdom, and to acquire for himself such a control over them, as would drive his antagonist from the helm, and render his own political services indispensable. His splendid eloquence, which filled to overflowing the Cathedral of Notre Dame, his well-simulated zeal for religion and for the interests of his diocese, his unremitting ministrations among the poor of his flock, his profuse liberalities—to supply which he borrowed enormous sums—won for him complete sway over his clergy, and over the citizens and the populace of the capital. Endowed with extraordinary genius, devoured by restless ambition, unfettered by moral restraints, possessing in an unrivalled degree the talents of a demagogue —the dangerous faculty of swaying multitudes, and moulding their fickle passions to his own purposes—sustained by a resolute audacity, and a readiness of resource equal to every emergency, he secretly bent all the great powers of his mind, and used all the expedients of his art, to kindle, and, at the same time, rule in his own interests the nascent spirit of disaffection. Proceeding with wary steps, he preserved amicable relations with the Queen and the Prime Minister. He kept up confidential communications with Condé, with the discontented nobles, with Madame de Chevreuse in exile, with the most violent and therefore most popular members of the Chambers, whom he moved at will through the ascendency of a superior mind, and his influence over the meaner citizens; sounding the thoughts of all, and making the designs of each subservient to his own. Besides the leaders of Parisian democracy and the factious councillors with whom he held carefully-concealed conferences at the Archbishop's residence, he maintained intimate relations with plotters of a more dangerous character. Such were Fontrailles, Montresor, St. Ibal, men of infamous lives and desperate fortunes, the inferior agents in all the schemes for the assassination of Richelieu, whose whole existence had been a dark conspiracy against the public welfare. Nobles themselves, these men gave the Coadjutor command over numbers of the inferior nobility, needy and debauched adventurers, who, for the slightest hope of personal advantage, were ready to throw themselves into any enterprise, no matter how perilous or criminal. A confirmed libertine, and though one of the ugliest and most ungraceful men in France, enjoying the favours of the most celebrated beauties of the time, De Retz had the art of making his mistresses zealous agents in his schemes. At the same time the most devout women in Paris, charmed by his fervid preaching, and his ostentatious charities, trumpeted his virtues, everywhere, with credulous enthusiasm. And yet, notwithstanding his many vices and his reckless selfishness, De Retz would probably have made one of the most admirable ministers France ever possessed. His mind had been enlightened and enlarged by deep study of the great writers of antiquity, whom he often rivalled in the elevation of his thoughts, and the elegance of his style. He was a profound observer of the men and the events of his own time, and he was probably the only French statesman, not of plebeian blood, who knew the value of popular rights, and had a genuine sympathy with rational freedom. His ambition, though unscrupulous, was not altogether ignoble. He loved France; he believed that he was the most capable to guide her destinies, and he aspired to link his name with her greatness. Had he succeeded in grasping firmly the helm of affairs, like Julius Cæsar, the great model upon whom he formed his life, he would perhaps have blinded the world to the crimes and follies of his youth by the splendour of his later career.

The Duke of Bouillon, a political leader of the highest rank, who played a part only second in importance to that of De Retz in the drama of the Fronde, was by birth a sovereign prince, and one of the greatest nobles of France; and by nature a remarkable man in an age fertile in extraordinary characters. His father, Henri de la Tour d'Auvergne, Viscount of Turenne, chief of a powerful and ancient family in the South of France, and one of the most valiant captains of Henry of Navarre, had obtained from his sovereign in recompense for his services the hand of Charlotte de la Marck, heiress of the Duchy of Bouillon, and of the independent principality of Sedan. His wife dying without issue, he married again, the sister of Prince Maurice of Nassau, who, after the death of the Duke of Parma, was esteemed the greatest general of his age. From this illustrious alliance sprang two sons, the subject of this sketch, and his still more famous brother, Marshal Turenne. The youth of Bouillon had been cradled in intrigue, and his powerful intellect had been precociously matured by the stimulating atmosphere of political strife in which the mighty spirit of Richelieu lived and ruled. An aristocrat of the purest type, and a Huguenot chief, there was scarcely a conspiracy against the great minister in which Bouillon had not borne a principal part; but his almost impregnable fortress of Sedan, conveniently situated on the confines of the French and Spanish dominions, afforded him a secure refuge in reverse. He was at length arrested at the head of his troops when in command of a French army in Italy, for complicity in the treason of Cinq-Mars, and was allowed by Richelieu, at the earnest intercession of the Prince of Orange, to ransom his life by ceding Sedan to the French Crown. Since the period of this compulsory sacrifice, all his energies had been vainly directed to recover his forfeited territory, or obtain an equivalent grant of lands or money. Long cozened by Mazarin with illusory hopes, self-interest and resentment urged him to espouse the popular cause. Few men of his time were so highly gifted by nature with the qualities that achieve success in a turbulent age. He was cool, skilful, and far-seeing. He had at command an unstudied yet artful eloquence, equally potent to convince a council of statesmen or to sway a popular assembly. His abilities for civil affairs were of the first order; his military talents were little inferior to those of his illustrious brother. At a subsequent period of his life, during the exile of Cardinal Mazarin from France, he became the chief adviser of the Regent, and his premature death relieved the Cardinal of a most formidable rival. Although his general policy was deeply leavened by the selfishness that characterised his age and his order, he displayed on many occasions noble and generous qualities which do not always survive in a mind, no matter how fine and chivalrous its original feelings, which from infancy has breathed the tainted air, and been nurtured amidst the seething passions of a corrupt and factious era.

The gallant and accomplished Prince of Marsillac, better known by his later title of Duke of la Rochefoucault, was another great noble who played a brilliant part in the Fronde, of which he has left us such a vivid picture in his "Memoirs." Although yet young, he had been the ablest of the party styled the " Importants," with the exception of Chateauneuf. But the cynical temper and the fastidious hauteur already observed in the future author of " The Maxims " detracted from his qualifications as a political leader. At the time of the downfall of his party he had deliberately forfeited the distinguished favour of Anne of Austria, due to him for chivalrous devotion at a season of great peril, and splendid prospects of employment, rather than betray his principles or desert his old friend Madame de Chevreuse. He occasionally appeared at Court after his partial disgrace, but was treated by the Regent with coldness and neglect; and he amused the leisure to which her ingratitude condemned him by literary pursuits, and by noting keenly the course of events. Like Bouillon, la Rochefoucault knew nothing of the lofty and Catholic sentiment of patriotism that animated Molé. A proud descendent of the Frankish conquerors, the great majority of the nations were only to him the descendents of the vanquished Gauls; Frenchmen, indeed, by name, but of an alien and inferior race, doomed to perpetual exclusion from high political or military trust, to wear for ever the badges of subjection. Obedience to the King, within the limits imposed by fidelity to his order and to his friends, was his rule of public duty. Following this narrow law of political conduct, he had generously rejected the splendid offers of Richelieu through friendship for Anne of Austria, and those of Anne of Austria through friendship for Madame de Chevreuse. His mortal foe, De Retz, accuses him of habitual deceit, masked by a show of candour; and he himself acknowledges that he used the affection of the beautiful Madame de Longueville to further his political designs. But no man of his party who took part in the troubles of the time was governed by a higher sense of honour, or was less swayed by selfish devotion to purely personal ends. His birth, his principles, his disposition, should have made him the prop and ornament of the throne; in the strange confusion of the political world his brilliant qualities and even his loyal character made him a tower of strength to faction.

Gaston, Duke of Orleans, occupies an unenviable eminence among those public men, without strength or dignity of character, upon whom the unhappy accident of birth or circumstance thrusts a greatness that only serves to expose, in the strongest light, failings to which the pitiless finger of history directs the everlasting contempt of mankind. He was the only brother of Louis XIII., and had been till near the close of that sickly and unpopular monarch's· reign heir presumptive to the French Crown. The spoiled darling of his mother, Mary of Medicis, the hope of France in her impatient writhings under an iron despotism, and possessing, in a considerable degree, the external graces and the superficial accomplishments which adorn a Court, and win popular applause, a very moderate share of political virtue and capacity would have ensured to him the second place in the kingdom in influence as well as in rank. But no advantages of fortune, no indulgent partiality of his countrymen, could supply an utter absence of sterling worth, or shield a nature so frivolous from just discredit. Throughout his life, he appears to have been incapable of forming an independent resolution, or of consistently adhering to any line of conduct, no matter how obviously conducive to his own interests, which the influence of a stronger mind had forced him to adopt. Morally, perhaps physically, a coward, his notorious falseness resulted from excessive timidity rather than from natural depravity. He was cursed with a restless, though impotent, love of faction, without being gifted with the qualities which render faction formidable. The fatuity with which he suffered himself to be hurried into rash and criminal enterprises was on a par with the vacillation which in the hour of action paralysed his faculties and wrecked the efforts of his friends, and with the abject meanness by which he avoided the consequences of his folly. Ever the dupe of his own egregious vanity, ever shamelessly servile to the caprices or guilty ambition of some designing favourite, whom he as shamelessly betrayed at the approach of danger, he had lent to every conspiracy against his brother's authority the sanction of his support, and had invariably sacrificed his accomplices to his own safety. He abandoned

his mother, and the gallant nobles who were ever
but too ready to respond to his call, to the vengeance of Richelieu, with the selfish indifference of
a mind for which secure infamy alone had no
terrors. Louis XIII. extended to him to the
last an indulgent forbearance, which was probably
prompted as much by disdain as by natural partiality; but no ties of affection, gratitude, or honour
could bind his fickle disposition. He only ceased to
trouble the State when he had sunk so low in
public esteem as to be no longer able to inspire
trust, and when the strong arm of Richelieu had
struck down all whose support could lend importance to his opposition. After the annulling of
his brother's will had shorn his office of Lieutenant
General of the kingdom of nearly all its independent powers, Orleans remained in the condition of a
political cypher, until the breaking out of new dissensions in the State afforded fresh scope to his
feverish incapacity. It then appeared that years,
without bringing him wisdom, had confirmed and
given a ludicrous development to his constitutional
timidity. In every difficulty he shrank from committing himself to a definite line of conduct, as a
child shrinks from the goblin terrors with which
its fancy peoples a darkened chamber; and he
resorted to a somewhat similar mode of escape, it
being his habit, when importuned for a decision, to

bury himself for days together in bed, until the danger had passed away. Yet, notwithstanding an impotence and a craven selfishness of character, which could not fail to provoke scorn, Gaston, throughout the greater part of his life, was eminently popular. His manners, gracious and affable, captivated the multitude. His restless craving after importance, combined with an uneasy consciousness of real insignificance, inclined him to assume an air of patronage towards the popular party; and he was gifted with a natural flow of eloquence, which, when not checked by unworthy fears, charmed the turbulent passions of a revolutionary age. His talents and his defects, his royal birth and his high office, to which the course of events might restore all its original authority, rendered him a formidable, though treacherous tool for the hands of an able demagogue.

The advantages of a close union with Orleans did not escape De Retz, when he had relinquished the hope of supplanting Mazarin in the Regent's favour. Before long the versatile genius and the resolute will of the accomplished prelate had secretly acquired a hold, unprecedented in strength and duration, on the fickle mind of the Lieutenant General; an ascendency fraught with grave political consequences.

The extraordinary escape of the Duke of

Beaufort from the high donjon keep of the Castle of Vincennes set loose another antagonist of the Government, whose opposition appears to have been anticipated by the Cardinal with nervous apprehension. The mental calibre of Beaufort was not by any means powerful; but alone of the House of Vendôme he had inherited the enterprising spirit and the popular manners of his grandfather, Henry IV. He was the hero of the populace, and especially of the fishwomen of Paris, and a rigorous imprisonment of five years had exasperated, to the last degree, his old animosity against Mazarin. Some remains of former partiality for her handsome young champion, some feeling of remorse for the terrible fate which had overtaken his headstrong folly, led the Regent to receive the intelligence of his flight with equanimity. She resisted the pressing advice of her minister to have him pursued to his father's chateau of Anet, whither he had retired. Beaufort, finding himself unmolested in his retreat, opened communications with his old confederates and with De Retz, impatient for any enterprise which promised him the excitement of bold action and revenge.

In a society so pregnant with elements of discord, and containing men so able and so willing to set them in a blaze, a spark was sufficient to

cause a dangerous conflagration. A stretch of
authority, rash and ill-timed, but by no means
novel, on the part of the Regent, lit up the civil
war of the Fronde; so called in sarcastic allusion
to the conflicts waged with slings and stones by
the boys of Paris outside the city walls. During
the short suspension of political discussions at the
Palace of Justice, which had been conceded with
great reluctance to the earnest solicitations of the
Duke of Orleans, the Duke of Chatillon arrived
in Paris, bringing intelligence of Condé's great
victory at Lens. The Queen was transported with
joy, not so much on account of the defeat of the
Spaniards, as because she thought that the moment
had arrived for quelling the opposition of the
magistracy by a decisive blow. Contrary to the
opinion of Mazarin, who wished to await the expected coming of the Prince with a strong military
force, she determined, in her fierce impatience, to
brook no further delay in making some of the
more factious presidents and councillors belonging to the extreme party of the Chambers, who
shaped their proceedings in avowed emulation of
the Parliamentary leaders in England, feel the
weight of her anger. The most obnoxious of
these was an old councillor named Broussel,
poor, honest, of slender capacity, and Republican
opinions, whose violent harangues and simple life

attracted the love and admiration of the lowest class of citizens. These revered him as a model of patriotic virtue, and styled him their father. The foolish old man, when spouting sedition, was merely the mouth-piece of the Coadjutor. As often as it suited the policy of the scheming prelate to increase or give a new direction to the agitation of the public mind, he secretly inspired Broussel with the ideas he wished to have ventilated in the Palace of Justice.

The 26th of August, the day appointed for a religious service at Notre Dame, in public thanksgiving for the success of the French arms, was fixed upon in private conclave at the Palais Royal for the *coup d'état*. The King and the Regent, attended by the whole Court, proceeded in state to the Cathedral, the regiments of Guards lined the way, and were massed at convenient points along the route. The Parliament, the municipal authorities, and the other civil or ecclesiastical corporations of the capital were present in their robes of ceremony. The Coadjutor, assisted by a crowd of prelates blazing in the splendour of religious pomp, ministered at the altar, chaunted the Te Deum, and consecrated the captured standards; and at the conclusion of the service the royal *cortége* returned quietly to the Palace. So well had the design of the Regent been cloaked by her placid serenity, and by the benevolent professions of the Cardinal, that even the lynx-eyed vigilance of the Coadjutor was lulled to rest. The first circumstance that awakened suspicion was the unusual spectacle of Comminges, Lieutenant of the Swiss Guards, whose duty it was to precede his sovereign, lingering in the church after the King's departure. The ominous news was whispered from bench to bench. A panic seized the ranks of the Parliament. They rushed forth pell-mell through all the doors, and in the struggle and confusion the magistrates, marked out for the vengeance of the Government, effected their escape, with the exception of the President Blancmesnil, who was hurried off to Vincennes. Comminges then went, preceded by a coach and a strong escort, in search of Broussel, who lived in a mean house, in a narrow squalid street by the river. The old councillor had absented himself from the religious ceremony, and was found in his dressing-gown and slippers at dinner with his family. Terror at the sight of the King's Lieutenant deprived him of speech or motion, and he was dragged off by Comminges, somewhat unceremoniously, and flung into the coach. But in the meantime an old female domestic had rushed, with shrieks and wild gestures, to an open window, and filled the air with her cries, " To the rescue

of Broussel, the Father of the People." The
bargemen from the neighbouring wharves, and
the whole ragged population, male and female, of
the dingy alleys which crowded the quarter,
roused by her appeals, swarmed forth in fury,
armed with every weapon their rage could find.
Stones, brickbats, and domestic utensils rained
upon the escort. The carriage was smashed to
pieces; but after a series of desperate combats,
Comminges, by the timely succour of a fresh
body of guards, was enabled to carry off his
prisoner to St. Germain.

The blow by which the Regent hoped to crush
sedition in the Chambers had now fallen, though
with only partial success; but the consequences of
this act of violence were far different from what
she had anticipated. In her blind anger she saw
not, and recked not, how thoroughly the whole
body of society was quickened by the restless discontent which tossed and frothed on the surface;
that the blatant demagogues whom she had seized
were but puppets moved by the secret agency of
skilful hands. Hardly had she tasted its delights
when she was rudely awakened from her dream of
vengeance by the armed hand of revolt. In an
incredibly short time all Paris was in arms.
Insurrection bristled in every street, and the tide
of the living sea, forcing its impetuous way over

the feeble obstacles that only excited its rage, choked up all the avenues of the Palais Royal.. De Retz, taken completely by surprise, and desirous of keeping on good terms with the Regent, set out on hearing of the commotion, without even taking time to put off his episcopal vestments, from the Cathedral to the Palace. On the Pont Neuf he saw Marshal la Meillerai with a handful of mounted guards beset by an angry mob, led on by Broussel's terrible old woman servant, and in imminent peril of being flung over the battlements into the river. The Marshal, in self-defence, had shot a porter, and the bleeding body excited the fury of the porter's comrades. The appearance of the Coadjutor somewhat calmed the tumult. Borne, amidst vociferous cheers, over the heads of the crowd, he knelt down in the mud and administered to the dying man the consolations of religion. Then, mounting the parapet of the bridge, he harangued the multitude, rescued the Marshal from their hands by promising to intercede with the Regent for Broussel, and proceeded to fulfil his mission, the vast throng kneeling for his benediction.

The Archbishop found Anne of Austria boiling with indignation. Contemning the clamour of insolent *canaille,* and suspecting the ambitious prelate—whose influence over the lower classes of Paris had been maliciously brought to her recollection, with injurious comments, by Mazarin—of fostering the outbreak, she received his advice and his proffers of service with fierce displeasure and menacing gestures, which all her powers of dissimulation were unable to control. She scoffed at his representations of danger, and declared that rather than release her prisoners she would strangle them with her own hands. At length, unable any longer to retain the slightest appearance of composure, she swept disdainfully from the presence chamber, and slammed the door of the little adjoining room to which she was accustomed to retire. The courtiers, though really uneasy, flattered the mood of their mistress. Some openly mocked at the astonished prelate; some paid him ironical compliments on his popularity with his flock; some imitated the cries of Broussel's beldame. De Retz, though incensed and alarmed at the demeanour of the Queen, yielded to the urgent entreaties, and even gentle violence of Orleans and Mazarin, who shuddered at the peril, and issued forth again with La Meillerai to pacify the insurgents.

The Marshal, who was a man of impetuous temperament, having mounted his horse, galloped among the crowd, brandishing his sword and shouting "Long live the King, liberty for Broussel."

The people in the distance, unable to catch his words, and mistaking his intentions, overwhelmed him and his escort with a shower of missiles. The soldiers fired with deadly effect, and pursued the flying multitude to an open space called the Croix de Trahoir, where they were swallowed up by converging torrents of the insurgents. In the meanwhile De Retz had been seized, and carried along with joyous shouts by a mud-grimed body of his admirers into the *mêlée*, where the blow of a stone, behind the ear, felled him to the ground. As he lay partially stunned, an infuriated ragman presented a pistol to his head in order to blow out his brains. With admirable presence of mind he exclaimed, " Hold, wretch; ah! if your father only saw you." The ragman, shocked at the idea of killing his father's friend, looked at his victim, recognised the Archbishop, and, stricken with horror at the crime he had been about to commit, uttered penitential howlings. The multitude, attracted by the cries, hurried eagerly to the spot, permitting La Meillerai a second time to escape. Tenderly raising De Retz, they bore him back to the palace "to tell Madame Anne the will of the people."

The Coadjutor again pressed upon the Regent the necessity of conceding the popular demands, and was warmly supported by la Meillerai, who bore grateful testimony to the great and perilous services De Retz had rendered the Crown, and to the irresistible force of the insurrection. But Anne of Austria, more enraged than ever, and confirmed in her unjust suspicions by the evident sway the Coadjutor exercised over her rebellious subjects, repaid his exertions with bitter reproaches, and rejected his counsels with scorn and defiance. The vague promises which terror extorted from the Cardinal he knew to be worthless. Making the most of these, however, and assisted by the promptings of hunger and the approaching night-fall, he prevailed on the majority of the insurgents to disperse. Then, faint with fatigue, long fasting, and the pain of severe contusions on his head and side, he returned to the Archiepiscopal Palace.

When De Retz reached home, his mind became a prey to the most gloomy emotions; the evident dislike of the Regent wounded his vanity, and dashed down the ambitious hopes he had founded on her former favour; her resentful distrust, so ungrateful, and so unfounded in the present emergency, cut him to the soul, and filled him with dark forebodings. As he tossed restlessly on his couch, racked by anguish of mind and body, one of his friends, arriving from the Palais Royal, brought him intelligence that the Court was flushed with extravagant exultation at the rapid dispersion of the insurgents, and that his own adventures during the day had been an acceptable theme of jest and sarcastic comment at the Regent's supper. Later on, a message was brought to him from Marshal la Meillerai warning him to provide for his safety, as it had been determined to exile him to Quimper, to shut up Broussel in the citadel of Havre, and to banish the Parliament to Montargis. Starting up with an oath, he inveighed against the folly and ingratitude of the Court, and vowed before the following night to have all Paris at his feet.

The capital was divided into sixteen sections, in each of which the substantial citizens were regularly mustered and trained to arms, under officers chosen by themselves. The Regent and Mazarin, in their ignorance of the disposition of the middle classes, relied with confidence on the loyalty of the Municipal Guards, and had issued directions to them to assemble for the defence of order on the following day. In fact, although the burghers had assumed arms to protect their houses from pillage, they had hitherto remained inactive spectators of the movement to rescue Broussel. But the commanding officers of the principal quarters, and still more their wives, were devoted to De Retz; and the citizens generally, while anxious to protect their property from the rabble, were full of zeal for the Parliament and of hatred for Cardinal Mazarin. The Coadjutor sent for some of the leading inhabitants of the different sections, painted in the darkest colours the designs of the Government, and arranged with them the plan of a general insurrection. Then issuing forth at midnight, in the dress of a cavalier, he traversed the streets, rousing up his adherents in the chambers, and troubling the air with sinister rumours and vague alarms of approaching danger. At the same time his numerous aides-de-camp among the inferior nobles—the dark brood of social corruption, skilled from long practice in all the arts of sedition—penetrating in the guise of artizans the dens of poverty and crime in the neighbourhood of Notre Dame, and flitting about the watch-fires on the Quai des Orfevres, where bands of desperadoes bivouacked for the night, howling and dancing around the flames, spread disquieting reports regarding the fate of Broussel, and incited the populace to rescue or avenge him. Having laid the train and lit the match, De Retz returned home to await the explosion.

The tocsin rang out in loud peals through the different quarters. The alarmed citizens, rushing forth at the summons, learned with indignation from their leaders the perfidious projects of the detested Italian, and hastened to range themselves under the civic banners. The motley population of the poorer regions streamed forth again; some brandishing the implements of their crafts, some carrying broken match-locks, some clad in tarnished cuirasses, decorated with half-effaced emblems of the Holy League, or dragging along rusty pikes that had done service at Agincourt. Strong chains were drawn across the entrances of the streets, and barricades were piled up at every point of advantage. At five o'clock the Parliament assembled, decreed the arrest of Comminges and his accomplices, and the impeachment of the ministers; and resolved to proceed in a body to the Palais Royal, to demand the release of their colleagues.

In the meantime the Chancellor Seguier had been summoned at an early hour to the Palace, where he received from Mazarin a written mandate, with orders to deliver it without delay to the Parliament. His brother, the Bishop of Meaux, and his beautiful daughter, the Duchess of Sully, on being informed of the hazardous mission entrusted to him, insisted on accompanying him to share his danger. Their coach was stopped, amidst hostile manifestations at the first barricade. The Chancellor, resolute to discharge his duty at all risks, and hoping to accomplish the journey to the Palace of Justice unmolested on foot, alighted, and sent the carriage with his brother and daughter to await his arrival at the Hotel de Luynes. The Bishop and his niece found the mansion silent and closely-barred, and as they were still knocking for admittance, they perceived Seguier flying towards the Court-yard for his life, closely pursued by a savage mob. A sleepy woman-servant, moved by the cries and prayers of the Duchess, gave the fugitives entrance, and had barely time to show them a closet concealed in the pannelling of the hall, when the outer doors were burst in by the rabble with triumphant yells. The insurgents searched all the apartments, fired up the chimneys, and sounded the wainscoating with the butt-ends of their muskets, venting their rage in frightful threats and imprecations. The Chancellor, believing that his last hour was come, confessed to the Bishop of Meaux, and prepared to meet his fate. But before his pursuers were able to discover his hiding-place, they were dislodged by the attack of a body of the Swiss Guards, whom Marshal la Meillerai led to his rescue. The unhappy objects of the popular fury, having already tasted of the bitterness of death, set out again, under the protection of the troops, to encounter the baffled vengeance of their assailants. The mob, rallying in the streets, charged the escort, and riddled the carriage with a volley of musketry. The Duchess, struck by a bullet, fell insensible into her father's arms. But the Swiss fought their way gallantly through the press, and succeeded in placing the Chancellor and his family—more dead than alive—within the shelter of the Palais Royal. When Anne of Austria awoke at nine o'clock, it was to learn that the spent commotion, which she had contemptuously compared, on the preceding night, to a fire of straw, had burst forth again in universal and skilfully-organised revolt; that more than twelve hundred barricades, surmounted by the banners of her loyal companies, raised their menacing forms on every side of the Palace; and that one hundred thousand citizens were in arms to wrest the popular magistrates from her grasp.

The danger that gathered round the Regent, far from appalling her, only exasperated her pride. In vain the Governor of Paris, and such of the city authorities as remained faithful to their trust, rushing pale and breathless into her presence, in disordered and stained apparel which bore evidence to the perils they had encountered, warned her that the excited people were ready to trample her guards under foot, and to tear down the palace stone from stone. In vain

Orleans, Mazarin, and the crest-fallen courtiers, with tears in their eyes, implored her to yield. In vain Molé and his colleagues, who had marched in long procession from the Palace of Justice through the insurgent hosts, entreated her to save the realm from the catastrophe in which conflicting passions were about to plunge it. She vehemently reproached the First President with the seditious conduct of the Parliament, and denounced against it a vengeance which should be memorable to all succeeding times. Tears of rage and scorn gushed from her eyes at the pusillanimous desertion of her Council. But her own resolution never faltered; she declared she would never yield to the dictation of vile *canaille*. One ray of hope flashed across her gloomy meditations as she sat aloof in her little grey chamber—as her usual retiring room was called—calm upon her brow, fury and almost despair in her heart. Instinctively recognising in the formidable movement that so suddenly confronted her the master hand which had organised and impelled it, she sent for the Coadjutor. De Retz replied that he was her Majesty's very humble servant, but that the injuries he had received, in her service, on the previous day rendered him unable to leave his bed.

In the meantime the Parliament had set out, on their return to the Palace of Justice, in order to deliberate on the Regent's answer to their petition. The magistrates were soon stopped and questioned by the ferocious populace, and being unable to announce the release of Broussel, had a narrow escape of being torn to pieces. Several of them casting away their robes, fled for their lives. Molé, incapable of fear, bore with undaunted composure the violence and insults, for which he was the especial mark. But, though unmoved at his own danger, he saw with patriotic anguish that the safety of the city, and even of the monarchy were at stake; and he slowly retraced his way to the Palais Royal, determined to break, by a supreme effort of his iron will, the unbending obstinacy of the Regent. Entering her presence again, he addressed her in words of stern remonstrance, to which her ears had long been unaccustomed. His passionate energy, the agonised apprehension for the fate of his young Sovereign that shook his intrepid nature, struck her dumb, and quelled her haughty spirit. In the lurid light which his burning eloquence threw upon the picture of impending ruin, she at length saw the terrible peril of the State. The Princesses of the Blood, and the ladies of her household, chilled with terror to the marrow of their bones, flung themselves at her feet and besought her to have pity on them. The unfortunate Queen of England, a penniless outcast in her native land, mournfully seconded their prayers, assuring Anne that the civil war which had laid her husband's throne in the dust had not worn such a terrible aspect, at the beginning, as this insurrection now presented. The cries and imprecations that rose nearer and more threatening in the air, told her, in language that could no longer be mistaken, that the stormy wave of revolution was fast sapping the foundations of the throne. She felt the sceptre of Regency trembling in her grasp; she saw the crown tottering on the youthful brow of her son; and, burning with shame and indignation, yielded to inexorable necessity. Royal carriages were despatched to bring back the liberated magistrates to their homes. The whole capital, frantic with joy, flocked to swell the triumphal entry of Broussel. The Parliament gave him a public reception, and then, on his proposal, decreed that the citizens should lay down their arms, and demolish the barricades. In a few hours the vast multitudes had quietly dispersed, traffic flowed again without impediment through its myriad channels, and every vestige of the revolt had disappeared. The whole struggle, so furious and so brief, rose and fell as if it were some magic spectacle that had started into life and vanished at successive waves of an enchanter's wand. This was the first act of the strange drama of the Fronde.

CHAPTER V.

THE rude lesson she had received from the popular party which she held in such contempt, without altering Anne of Austria's determination to uphold with a high hand all the arbitrary prerogatives of the Crown, taught her the value of Mazarin's prudent counsel not to attempt a blow at the Parliament until the presence of Condé, with his troops, enabled her to strike with decisive effect. All her hopes of triumph and revenge now rested on the Prince. The empire which the Cardinal had established over her mind and her affections was not, indeed, sensibly impaired. But she began almost involuntarily to distrust gentleness so little in unison with her own fierce passions; to doubt whether he possessed force and decision of character sufficient to oppose revolutionary violence. The rank, the principles, the imperious nature, the unrivalled military genius, and the repeated pledges of the victor of Lens led her to count upon him with confidence as the surest support and avenger of her outraged authority. Dissembling her feelings in order to gain time to concert a plan of operations with the Prince, she sent again for De Retz, upon whom the success of the outbreak seems to have acted as a sovereign restorative, received him with flattering professions of penitence and esteem, and requested him to pay the equally contrite Cardinal a visit of reconciliation. The Coadjutor found the minister in familiar conference with Broussel, heaping civilities on the bewildered old councillor, and was welcomed with open arms. But his political insight was too keen to be deceived a second time by the fair appearances of the Court. He saw that the struggle between the Regent and the Parliament—between Mazarin and himself—was only beginning. Distrusting the ability of the magistrates to withstand the Government, he secretly laboured with all his energy and skill to build up a mighty auxiliary confederacy of great nobles and popular leaders, of which he had already laid the foundations, and by means of which he intended to hurl his Italian rival from power, and to mount into his vacant seat.

Strange to say, the chief of the Fronde, who figured in his schemes, who was to give the new coalition cohesion and irresistible force, was the same personage on whom the Regent relied to dash it to pieces. The splendid genius of Condé had kindled in the mind of De Retz an ardent admiration, which the exasperation of disappointed hope, envenomed by a long and unsparing interchange of injuries and insults, was never able to extinguish. It was no secret to him how angrily the Prince chafed at the political ascendancy of Mazarin, and he had artfully fed this impatient humour by opening before Condé's ambition the prospect of unbounded sway during the minority of the King, if he would rid the kingdom of the low-born foreigner who monopolised the Regent's favour. With unscrupulous art, he secretly fomented the public hatred and distrust of the Government. Every day new rumours of hostile projects on the part of the Regent, some of them of the wildest extravagance, but all greedily devoured by popular credulity and suspicion, and all catching some colour of probability from the advance of troops towards the capital, provoked formidable tumults. On one occasion the Parisians were thrown into a paroxysm of terror by a report that the Queen of Sweden had arrived with an army of Amazons to avenge her sister sovereign. Every day ribald Mazarinades, and caricatures equally witty and coarse, depicting the amorous relations of Anne of Austria and her minister, were flung upon the seething capital from secret presses, to feed its ' rancorous and prurient humour. When the Regent went to visit a favourite convent or church, insulting verses, loudly chaunted by dishevelled demireps, assailed her ears. Her hours of repose were disturbed by continual alarms. Mazarin no longer dared to stir from the Palace. Distracted by apprehensions, he was incapable of giving his mistress advice, except to urge her departure from a scene of so much danger and discomfort. But she bided her time with the patience of deep hatred. When she considered her preparations sufficiently advanced, she sent the young King and the Cardinal quietly from the city, covered their retreat with admirable coolness, and then retired in open day to Ruel, the country house of the Duchess of Aiguillono. There she summoned Condé to join her.

The first step Anne of Austria took, when beyond the reach of popular sedition, left the magistrates without a doubt regarding the nature of her intentions. This was to order the arrest of Chavigny and Chateauneuf. Both of these statesmen, and especially Chavigny, were known to cultivate intimate relations with prominent members of the Parliament, and were objects of Mazarin's jealous aversion. Chavigny was shut up in the Castle of Vincennes, of which he had long been governor; Chateauneuf, less obnoxious to the Regent, was exiled to the province of Berri. The Parliament, restrained by Molé in observance of the pledge that had been given 'to Orleans, and renewed to the Regent when Broussel was set at liberty, had for some weeks forborne discussion upon the disputed prerogative of arbitrary arrest, with a tacit understanding of corresponding forbearance on the part of the Government. But the arrest of Chavigny and Chateauneuf, universally attributed to the perfidious counsels of the Cardinal, produced an explosion of rage in the Palace of Justice which swept away every tendency to moderation. The High Court returned the blow by passing a resolution to deliberate on its decree passed in 1622, after the murder of Concini, which forbade foreigners to accept office in France upon pain of death. It dispatched the First President, at the head of a deputation, to Ruel, to request the Regent to return to Paris with the King, and either to set the prisoners free or bring them to trial. The deputation was also commissioned to invite the Princes of the Blood to attend a sitting of the Chamber, at which the thorny question of arbitrary imprisonment was to be discussed.

The envoys were received by Anne of Austria at a public audience. Condé had arrived at Ruel;

had been welcomed with joyful pride by the Queen, with humble deference by the Cardinal, as the saviour of the Monarchy; and had renewed his professions of devoted loyalty. Orleans was seemingly full of zeal in her cause. Supported by the chiefs of the House of Bourbon she laughed the demands of the magistrates to scorn. The Princes also rejected their summons with menaces and disdain. Hopeless of a pacific solution, the deputation returned to Paris to assist in taking measures for the defence of the city.

But the somewhat extravagant manifestation of loyalty by Orleans and Condé, which had driven the magistrates to despair, cloaked much secret hesitation, and an under-current of private intrigue. The representations of De Retz had borne fruit in the Prince's mind; and the impressions of former conferences were deepened in a stolen visit, which he now paid the Coadjutor at Notre Dame. Although from principle a firm supporter of the throne, to which he stood in near succession; and although regarding the political pretensions of councillors of Parliament, and the factious violence of the Parisian rabble with as much amazement, anger, and contempt as Anne of Austria herself, it was neither his interest nor his wish to establish the foreign favourite in the seat of Richelieu. The part which

Anne designed for him, that of executing the policy shaped in the brain of her able minister, presented to his mind in every odious and humiliating aspect by the taunts of the keen-witted Parisians, revolted his pride. His family experience taught him to appreciate the suggestion of De Retz, that the recognition of the principle of individual liberty, which the Parliament demanded, might hereafter prove a safeguard for himself. When, therefore, the Regent, at the next sitting of the Council of State, having expatiated with acrimony on the rebellious spirit of the capital, confidently appealed to Condé to reduce it to submission, to her intense astonishment and mortification, instead of returning a ready assent, he started difficulties, spoke of conciliation, and ended by offering himself as a mediator between the Crown and the Parliament. Orléans, greatly relieved by this unexpected turn of affairs, promptly gave his voice for peace. No other member venturing to advocate a policy which seemed too bold for the fiery Prince, Anne of Austria broke up the meeting in silent indignation.

A resort to the sword for the purpose of cutting the political knot being now out of the question, Orleans and Condé were authorised as representatives of the King to discuss terms of accommodation with the Presidents Molé and De Mesmes, the delegates of the Parliament. The Presidents again submitted for acceptance the articles passed by the United Chambers in the Hall of St. Louis. Those confering on the High Court a partial control over the finances and freedom of debate, already allowed in a maimed form by the Regent, were admitted without much difficulty. But upon the article securing to every Frenchman the right of being interrogated by his legal judges within twenty-four hours after his arrest, she was as unyielding as ever. Though rendered almost powerless by the desertion of the Lieutenant-General and the other Princes of the Blood, she fought the battle of the prerogative single-handed, with stubborn resolution. Mazarin, however, seeing in the ebullitions of arrogant temper which continually troubled Condé's intercourse with the Parliamentary delegates, the presage of a speedy change in his policy, excited all his influence to induce his mistress to temporise. He soothed her scruples with assurances that a short experience of the insolence of the Parisian demagogues would drive the imperious Prince into the extremity of antagonism to the popular cause; that, even at the worst, the King, on attaining his majority, would not be bound by the acts of the Regency. Slowly yielding to the arguments of her far-seeing minister, Anne of Austria offered to concede immunity from arbitrary imprisonment to the magistrates, reserving the irresponsible dominion of the Crown over the princes and nobles. But Molé and De Mesmes, worthy champions of a beneficent principle, would not consent that any Frenchman, however high, or however mean, should be excepted from its protection.

On the 24th of October, 1648, all the articles passed in the Hall of St. Louis, embodied in a Declaration drawn up by Molé, were accepted without reserve by the Regent, after one of those terrible mental conflicts which rage only in strong, passionate natures, and ever leave behind them indelible traces of their fury. This celebrated Declaration was a noble charter of constitutional freedom, throwing, so far as was possible in the circumstances of that particular time, over the liberty and the property of Frenchmen, the shield of a legal guarantee; a noble monument to the enlightened patriotism, and the lofty courage of the great magistrates who framed it. On the same day the Treaty of Westphalia, concluded at Munster by securing the depression of the House of Austria, and the independence of the minor German States, elevated France to the leading place in Europe, and consecrated the triumph of Richelieu's foreign policy. It was a day memorable in the history of France, and memorable in the life of Condé; which should have linked his name in imperishable renown with the freedom, as well as with the greatness of his country. Happy would it have been for his fame had he continued to restrain his fiery genius to the paths of national glory and national felicity. Happy would it have been for France had she devoted but a small part of the energy and talent, of the blood and treasure, squandered in efforts to extend her supremacy abroad, to preserve and develop constitutional liberty at home.

The Treaty of Munster and the Declaration of October 24 were celebrated by public rejoicings, and by all the outward signs of a general reconciliation. The King and the Regent returned to Paris. Chavigny and Chateauneuf regained their liberty, and the Parliament silently receded from its menacing attitude towards Cardinal Mazarin. But the interval of partial tranquillity that followed was a period of passive hostility rather than of peace. Mortified pride and baffled vengeance consumed the heart of the Regent. She made little secret of the grief and abhorrence with which she viewed the concessions wrung from her, or of her determination, at a more favourable juncture, to free the royal authority from such ignominious fetters. The unexpected desertion of Condé especially galled her. She never thoroughly trusted him again. The proceedings at Ruel had riveted for ever the ascendancy of Mazarin over her mind and her affections. The Princes of the Blood, as bitter experience taught her, had each his own independent aims, and claimed to share her power during the minority of her son. Mazarin was her creature, bound to her by every bond of gratitude and hope; whose political existence was inseparable from her own; whose marvellous ability and sustaining sympathies were absolutely enlisted in her service.

The frank co-operation of Condé, however, was essential to the success of her policy. Dissembling her indignation, she employed all her art to win him from his connexion with the popular party, and continually assailed his self-love with flattering tokens of regard and confidence. The Cardinal listened to all the Prince's wishes with reverential submission. But this policy of complaisance soon brought Anne of Austria into angry collision with the Duke of Orleans, and led to her receiving a mortifying proof of the unpopularity of her Government.

Condé's brother, the Prince of Conti, a youth of stunted growth, physical and mental, and, of a timorous nature, had shown a predilection for an ecclesiastical career. It was the interest of the head of the family to encourage this desire; the august dignities and the rich benefices in the Church which would reward the piety of a Prince of the Blood being treated, under the dispositions of their father's will, as equivalent to the large revenues settled on the younger son, should he elect to remain a layman. Condé, therefore, asked the Regent to transfer to Conti the nomination for a Cardinal's hat, which had long been promised to the Abbé la Riviere, the reigning favourite of the Lieutenant-General. Anne of Austria complied with this request without hesitation, and offered to compensate La Riviere by making him Archbishop of Rheims. But the aspiring Abbé, looking upon an archbishopric as a splendid exile, scornfully rejected the proposal, and openly reproached Anne with ingratitude for his exertions in keeping his master steady to her cause. Orleans, goaded on by his wife and daughter, hotly espoused his favourite's quarrel. In an angry interview at the Palais Royal, he came to an open rupture with the Regent; and he retired from Court. Anne of Austria at first treated his ill-humour with indifference; but no sooner had the news of the quarrel spread over Paris than all the great nobles, and all the popular leaders, thronged to the Luxembourg to offer their support. When the Lieutenant-General

appeared in the streets, the people crowded round
his coach, filled the air with acclamations, and
loudly urged him to seize the King and depose
the Regent. Consternation filled the Palais
Royal. The Regent sent her incensed brother-in-
law the most pressing entreaties for a reconciliation, which he curtly rejected. Condé, alone of
the Court, was in a state of supreme satisfaction.
He doubled the guards at the Palace, and denounced Orleans and La Riviere as traitors. In
the height of the public agitation, the Duke,
stricken by a sudden panic at his own popularity,
and at the display of military force, betook himself to bed, and refused to hold any further communication with Anne of Austria. She, in her alarm,
regarded his feigned illness as a pretence to cloak
the workings of a formidable conspiracy. Entrenched in the Palais Royal or the Luxembourg,
each side expected the attack in mortal terror.
This ludicrous situation might have found a
tragical issue had not La Riviere, appalled by the
danger of being crushed to pieces in the shock of
such mighty forces, sought a private interview
with the trembling Mazarin. A few words of
explanation led to an arrangement. A seat in the
Privy Council, and the renewed promise of a red
hat appeased the wrath of the favourite. Monsieur,
being assured that the peril had blown over, and

that his importance was sufficiently vindicated, condescended to accept the Regent's explanations, and restored the appearance of public tranquillity by again attending the Court.

The undisguised preference of the Parisians for his cousin, whom he despised, and their want of appreciation of his own services, cooled Condé's favourable disposition towards the Constitutional party. As Mazarin had predicted, one or two visits to the Palace of Justice converted this coldness into bitter enmity. The suspicious bearing of the Regent, and the arts of the Coadjutor, kept alive a general feeling of uneasiness, which found expression in the exaggerated statements and the irritating language of the democrats of the Chambers. Condé's imperious tone, and disdainful manner in repressing the factious cavillings which invaded every department of the State, and even the household of the young King, in search of grievances, often fictitious or frivolous, provoked defiant and insolent retorts from some of the younger magistrates, which lashed him into fury. It was in vain that De Retz, who watched the fluctuations of his mind with anxiety, repeated every argument, which, by convincing his judgment, or stimulating his ambition, might prevent his serving the interests of Cardinal Mazarin. Bred up in deep veneration for royalty, his

haughty soul could not brook alliance with
the low-born demagogues who had bearded him
in the Parliament. "My name," he said, "is
Louis of Bourbon, and I do not wish to shake the
Crown." Had he consulted sound policy, and his
own dignity, he would have curbed his indignation, and co-operated with the patriotic Molé in
upholding the Declaration of October 24, in
opposing alike the excesses of faction and of
authority. With his position and prestige this
course was not merely feasible, it was the course
most consonant with his own honour and advantage.
But entrusted from his earliest youth with the
supreme conduct of the greatest undertakings;
having from the very first bound fortune to his
chariot-wheels; being accustomed to see his will
a law to all around him, he had never acquired
the habits of self-control and reflection, or the
steadiness of purpose which come from wrestling
with difficulties. His glorious intellect and his
clear judgment were the sport of unruly passions,
often as short lived as they were violent. His
friend Marshal Grammont, a staunch adherent of
the Court, represented to him, while still swayed
by intemperate anger at the language of a few
obscure Councillors, that by accomplishing the
designs of the Regent, he would command her
gratitude for ever, and place himself in a position

to become the arbiter of the Minister's fate. Hurried along by wayward and unreasoning humours, he not only broke off his relations with the Coadjutor, but hastened to abet Anne of Austria with all the ardour of selfish ambition and revenge, in crushing the Parliament and tearing up the Charter so recently extorted through his connivance.

The sanction of the Lieutenant General of the realm was necessary for the use of military force against the Capital. The mind of Orleans was still estranged from the Regent by the irritation of scarcely-healed grievances; his pride was swollen by his unbounded popularity with the citizens; and the tortures of a severe attact of gout rendered him unusually testy. But Anne of Austria, in assiduous visits to his sick couch, exerted the feminine blandishments and the force of will which had so long held him in control. The treacherous Duke, after a few uneasy mental pangs, not only betrayed the confiding affection of his faithful Parisians, but entered cordially and even eagerly into the Regent's project to chastise them with famine and the sword. Condé proposed, in secret council at the Palais Royal, that the Court should retire to the Arsenal, which adjoined the Bastille, and thence issue a decree of exile against the Parliament. If the magistrates offered resistance, he undertook to enter the city at the head of his troops, sweep the streets with his artillery, and clear the Palace of Justice at the point of the bayonet. This bold plan of operations, which promised prompt and decisive success in the hands of a great soldier, was warmly approved by the Regent. But Orleans and Mazarin were terrified at the risks of discomfiture in a street fight. Anne of Austria, reluctantly yielding to their timid remonstrances, agreed to resort to the slower, though, in reality, more hazardous, measure of a blockade.

In the meantime De Retz had not been idle. The alienation of Condé, and the embarrassed demeanour of Monsieur warned him of the danger that was brewing. Having no faith in the ability of the Parliament to resist the Government, supported by the greatest general of the age and the soldiers of Lens, he had succeeded in banding together the chiefs of the great aristocratic houses in a secret league; and he treated for assistance with the Archduke Leopold at Brussels, through Madame de Chevreuse. The Princes of Vendôme, the Dukes of Bouillon, Elbœuf, and Longueville, the Prince of Marsillac, with their allies and dependents in the provinces, were prepared by his address to draw their swords for the Parliament. He and they were guided by animosity and interest to a common goal, the destruction of Cardinal Mazarin, and perhaps the deposition of the Regent, by means of an armed confederacy, ostensibly organised for the defence of the Declaration of the 24th of October. But in order to secure the stability and the harmonious action of the league against the jealous rivalries of so many proud magnates, it was necessary to place at its head a Prince of the Blood. Condé, whose adhesion to it was a cardinal point in his policy, had broken through his meshes. Orleans had also abandoned the Parliament. It seemed more than doubtful whether the timid Conti could be induced to venture into open opposition to his fiery brother.

Revolving this difficulty in his mind, De Retz went one day to visit Madame de Longueville. The beautiful and accomplished Duchess was at that time on very bad terms with the Regent, and with her elder brother. She was devoured by an ambitious fancy to shine in the sphere of politics. But, although brilliant and cultivated, she was not formed of sufficiently stern stuff for the *rôle* she coveted. Plastic under the influence of love, as clay in the hands of the potter, her opinions were swayed by her affections, and whoever engrossed her heart also governed her mind, and directed the current of her ideas in the channel of his own interests. With the Regent, she had never been a favourite. Anne of Austria found the languishing airs of the spoiled beauty, and *bel esprit* of the Hotel Rambouillet insufferable, and delighted in inflicting on her petty mortifications. Condé was said to have never forgiven her for revealing to his father the foolish project he had formed of marrying Mademoiselle Vigean. His conduct towards her at this period was singularly harsh and unfeeling. He treated her political pretensions with pitiless ridicule, and publicly inveighed, in unmeasured terms, against her gallantries, counselling her husband to shut her up for life in one of his castles. Madame de Longueville therefore lived retired from the Court in sullen discontent. Her younger brother Conti worshipped her with almost idolatrous love. Her husband, though not in the most intimate relations with her, was blessed with an indulgent disposition which rendered him incapable of treating her with severity. Already dissatisfied with the Government for refusing him the custody of the fortresses of Havre and Pont de l'Arche in Normandy, the sarcasms of the Prince, upon the subject of his wife's infidelity, only served to wound his pride, and embitter his resentment. It needed but a few artful hints, thrown out without apparent purpose by the Coadjutor, to conjure up before Madame de Longueville's imagination a dazzling vision of triumphant ambition and gratified vengeance. The prospect that arose before her of dividing the allegiance of France with Anne of Austria as Queen of the Fronde, of at once baffling her imperious brother, and wounding him where his pride was most exquisitely sensitive, by arraying against him the members of his own family in league with the demagogues of the capital, filled her with joy which no words could paint. She embraced the subtle prelate's schemes with rapture, engaged to remain behind in Paris, in the expected contingency of the Regent's departure, and pledged herself for the adhesion of Conti, of her husband, and of the Prince of Marsillac, to the cause of the Parliament.

De Retz found an equally enthusiastic and still more energetic ally in the Duchess of Bouillon. For the rare combination of beauty, bewitching grace, winning manners, and lively talents, this charming conspirator had few rivals; and she was distinguished besides by the unusual characteristic of unblemished fidelity to her husband. Her animosity towards Anne of Austria was intense, in consequence of the Regent having betrayed to Cardinal Richelieu the secret of the conspiracy of Cinq-Mars, which cost Bouillon his principality of Sedan, and had nearly cost him his head. By birth a subject of Spain, Madame de Bouillon maintained close relations with the Court of Brussels, of which she had been one of the brightest ornaments. Brave, ardent, self-sacrificing, and full of resources, she schemed, plotted and even coquetted with untiring energy, in concert with her lord, for the purpose of obtaining the satisfaction of his claims. She now established an intimate political liason with De Retz, who, while confessing in his memoirs the power of her fascinations, bears unimpeachable testimony to her singular virtue.

It was not in the nature either of Anne of Austria or of Condé to sleep upon a bold resolution deliberately adopted. They acted with a promptitude and secrecy which disconcerted the Coadjutor, and well-nigh frustrated all his plans. The measures resolved upon at the Palais Royal were veiled with profound dissimulation. Orleans, carefully guarded by La Riviere, now in close alliance with Mazarin, did not drop a hint of what was coming even to his wife. Condé was equally reticent with his idolised mother, whose existence was bound up in his. At the customary public receptions on New Year's Day, 1649, the gracious demeanour of the Regent was the subject of general comment and congratulation among the members of the High Court. On the 5th of January

Marshal Grammont entertained the Court. Anne of Austria passed the evening at the Palais Royal in pleasant conversation with her household. Vague rumours, that had somehow got afloat, of her intended flight from the Capital, appearing to disquiet some of her ladies, she made them a subject of mirth, mocking, in merry humour, at the absurd fears of the Parisians. At her usual hour, dismissing her retinue, she retired to bed. When all was quiet, after midnight, she rose again, roused up a few confidential attendants, and ordered the King and his brother to be dressed. Leading her sons by the hand, she left the palace by a secret staircase, traversed the gardens, and entering a coach that waited at a private entrance, drove through the city gates, and halted at a short distance without the walls. In the meantime Orleans, Condé, and Mazarin quitted the Hotel de Grammont together on foot. The Cardinal repaired without delay to join his mistress. Orleans, proceeding to the Luxembourg, awoke his wife, who received his commands to prepare for a journey in a very refractory spirit. Condé went to his family hotel, called up his mother and wife, and dragged the reluctant Conti out of bed. By three o'clock in the morning all the Royal family, with the exception of Madame de Longueville, who, pleading pregnancy, had refused to stir, were assembled together, in no very sociable temper, in the Regent's capacious coach, on their way to St. Germain.

The weather was bitterly cold. In the narrow domestic economy of that time, the King of France, though master of many spacious palaces, seems to have possessed only one complete set of furniture. When he changed his residence, that which he left was dismantled and deserted; and the Royal moveables accompanied the Court in huge baggage-waggons. No preparations having been made at the Chateau of St. Germain, for fear of exciting suspicion, the Royal party found it destitute of food, of fuel, and of the common necessaries of habitation. The resources of the little neighbouring village were inadequate to supply their simplest wants. A few mattresses, one of which Orleans appropriated to himself, and a small quantity of the humblest fare were procured with difficulty. Bread rose to famine prices. Straw was sold at a fabulous rate. The wood, hastily cut in the forest, was green, and would not burn. During the first twenty-four hours after their arrival the majority of the ladies and gentlemen, so hastily torn from their luxurious quarters in Paris, fasted, shivered, and watched in the damp and desolate rooms.

Anne of Austria, before quitting the Palais

Royal, had addressed letters to the great public bodies of the capital and the leading members of the nobility, charging the Parliament with treasonable designs against the King's person. The nobles were ordered instantly to repair to St. Germain, and it was announced that the Royal Armies were marching on the capital. The news spread like wildfire, throwing the populace into a paroxysm of rage and terror. Armed mobs seized the city gates, took possession of the waggons that were bearing away the King's effects, and would have pillaged the Palais Royal and the Palais Mazarin had not the Parliament placed these buildings under the charge of its own officers. The sight of crowds of panic-striken courtiers, choking up all the avenues of exit in their hurry to escape to St. Germain, added to the popular exasperation. But the majority of the magistrates and substantial citizens were chilled with dismay. The desertion of Orleans, who had promised to defend them against the evil practices of "Madame Anne," particularly depressed them. Yet such was the affection which the false Duke inspired, that while a Decree of the High Court forbade the removal of a single article from the Royal palaces or the Hotel Mazarin, carriages bearing the arms of Monsieur were allowed passage through the gates without question.

The desponding fears that weighed down the Parisian middle class filled De Retz with apprehension. All the confederate nobles, with the exception of the Duke of Bouillon, were still in the provinces, busy with their preparations for the coming struggle. Bouillon was proud, wary, and almost morbidly jealous of his shadowy dignity of sovereign prince. Suspecting trickery, and disdaining the companionship of greasy citizens, he listened to the explanations of the Coadjutor in very bad humour, refused to commit himself by any overt act in the absence of a Prince of the Blood, and even showed some disposition to repair to Court. Madame de Longueville received the disheartened prelate in tears. She had just been apprised that her irresolute husband, on his way up from Normandy to join her, had stopped at St. Germain. It was agreed that she should send the Marquis of Noirmoutier with letters to him and the Prince of Conti. De Retz, seeing in the evident desire for an accommodation that pervaded the minds of the magistrates, and in the absence of his high-born allies, the possible collapse of his schemes, began to think of his own safety. He had received orders to attend the Court, and he now thought it prudent to feign obedience. Setting out with great pomp from Notre Dame, he proceeded slowly through the most crowded streets, and, with tears rolling down his dejected face, showered his benedictions on the crowds who were attracted by his equipage. The people clamoured, and stopped his horses; but he besought them, in tones of anguish, not to expose themselves to the wrath of incensed majesty by arresting his journey, and detaining him to share their perils. His words had the desired effect. The postillions were dragged from their seats, the horses were unharnessed, and De Retz, elevated on a dray, was escorted back in triumph to his palace by a body-guard of shrill-tongued viragoes, while a band of sister furies shrieked and danced around the burning fragments of his coach. On reaching home, he addressed a submissive letter to the Regent, deploring his inability to obey her commands.

While the Chambers still hesitated between submission and defiance, a letter arrived in the King's name, exiling the Parliament to Montargis. The High Court, having been forewarned of its contents, resolved that out of respect for the Royal Authority the mandate should be deposited, unopened, in their Registry; and despatched Omer Talon and the other law officers of the Crown to learn from the Queen the names of the false accusers, who had calumniated her loyal companies. The deputation was compelled to halt before it reached

St. Germain ; was kept waiting for several hours of an inclement night, on the top of a bleak hill, exposed to a violent snow storm ; and was then sternly denied audience. This injurious treatment of their envoys showed the incensed magistrates that there only remained to them disgraceful submission or vigorous resistance. Casting aside their irresolution, they issued a decree declaring Cardinal Mazarin a public enemy, and the author of all the disorders of the realm, and denouncing against him the penalties of outlawry if found within the kingdom after the expiration of eight days.

Having lifted up the gage of battle, the High Court convoked a great council of all the notabilities of Paris to consider measures of defence. The meeting was attended by the Duke of Montbazon, Governor of the City, the Provost of the Merchants, and every person eminent in his public or private capacity, with the exception of the Duke of Bouillon, and the Military Governor, Marshal la Mothe Houdincourt, who declined to declare themselves, unless countenanced by a Prince of the Royal Family.

The burgher guard, with its reserve of partially drilled artizans, numbered about twenty thousand men. But the prosperous middle-aged tradesmen, who chiefly composed it, not being physically well adapted for feats of active warfare, it was decided that this force should be employed in the defence of the gates and ramparts, and of public order; and that an army of fourteen thousand foot and five thousand horse, of more mettlesome materials, should be levied for offensive operations. In order to provide funds for the campaign, the Parliament issued orders to the collectors of revenue throughout the kingdom to pay the proceeds of the taxes into the Hotel de Ville. It also imposed a house-tax on the Capital; every mansion with a *porte-cochere* being assessed at one hundred and fifty francs, shops and the meaner habitations at thirty francs each. The magistrates contributed with extraordinary generosity, and the Coadjutor undertook to equip and maintain a regiment at his own expense.

These bold proceedings produced a signal effect both at Paris and St. Germain. The citizens were roused from their despondency to the highest pitch of ardour. The Regent was wild with anger; but Mazarin's spirit quailed. He had no real friends even amongst the courtiers, who, finding that the hostile decrees launched against him, breathed respectful loyalty to the sovereign, began to give him cold looks, and to whisper to each other, that his was the malign influence that troubled the peace of the realm. Many of the nobles, who, although secretly disaffected, had gathered around the Regent, plucked up courage to avow their true sentiments. The example was set by the Duke of Elbœuf, a Prince of the house of Lorraine. Quitting the Court in the open day, he entered Paris, offered himself to the Parliament as their General, and was welcomed with acclamations.

This event was by no means pleasing to De Retz. He now felt certain of the speedy arrival of Condé and Longueville; and the aspiring aims and sudden popularity of the Lorraine Prince threatened to mar his schemes. He spent the day in spreading abroad sinister reports that Elbœuf was an agent of the Regent. After he had retired to rest, word was brought to him that the chiefs he so impatiently expected were vainly seeking admittance at one of the city gates. They had galloped off from St. Germain in the evening, but the burgher guard, ignorant of the intrigues of the Coadjutor, naturally looked upon the brother and brother-in-law of Condé as enemies, and planted a cannon against them. The rejected leaders passed many hours in a forlorn condition, exposed to the double danger of being blown to pieces by the insurgents, and of being captured by a detachment of the royal troops. At length De Retz, arriving with old Broussel, with great difficulty persuaded the suspicious citizens to give them entrance.

It was now four o'clock in the morning.

The Coadjutor carried Conti to the Palace of Justice, to offer his services to the Parliament. Conti's rank rendered this step equivalent to a demand of the supreme military command. But the timid boy, already scared by the responsibilities of his novel position, was dismayed by a chilling reception from the magistrates. The First President had just prevailed on the Chamber, despite the vehement opposition of the Coadjutor's friends, to elect Elbœuf General. The great magistrate suspected the correspondence of De Retz with the Archduke Leopold. He entirely distrusted the support of the feudal magnates, whom he knew from experience to be ever ready to sacrifice the public interests to their own. It was the policy of the Parliament to maintain in its integrity the authority of the Crown within the limits marked out by the Declaration of October; to defend it from the assaults of discontented nobles and interested agitators in league with the enemies of the kingdom. In order that the High Court might not be pushed beyond the legitimate bounds of self-defence, or compromised by schemes abhorrent to its principles, it was of the utmost importance that its General should be a servant loyally obedient to its wishes; not a master who would use it without its consent for the promotion of ulterior ends. Elbœuf, in open antagonism with De Retz and the feudal party, promised to be far more amenable to Parliamentary control than Conti, who was their puppet. When, therefore, Elbœuf, in reply to his rival's challenge, boldly declared he would never resign the dignity conferred on him, he was greeted with loud applause, and the crest-fallen Conti retired in discomfiture.

The gravity of the crisis was fully recognised by the Coadjutor and his allies. None of the aristocratic chiefs would consent to serve under Elbœuf. They held Council in the Hotel de Bouillon to concert measures for compelling the High Court to rescind its appointment, and for cowing the obnoxious General into submission. Bouillon, roused from his sullen lethargy by the remonstrances of De Retz, consented to take an active part in the proceedings.

The Parliament assembled at an early hour on the following morning, the elated Elbœuf sitting in pride of place by the side of the First President. Conti entered alone, and quietly took his seat. Shortly afterwards the Duke of Longueville, who was not a peer of France, craved audience, and was conducted to a place. In a short speech he placed all the resources of his Government of Normandy at the service of the Chamber, and announced that his wife and children were about to take up their abode in the Hotel de Ville as hostages for the fidelity of the Prince of Conti and himself. His words created an extraordinary sensation. Before the agitation had time to subside, the Duke of Bouillon slowly entered the Chamber, leaning on the shoulders of two gentlemen, with great parade of gout. In a few blunt sentences, he declared that he would joyfully defend the cause of the Parliament under such an illustrious prince as Conti. His speech called up Elbœuf in hot assertion of his rights. Accusation and retort were freely bandied about. In the midst of the uproar, Marshal la Mothe, Military Governor of Paris, arrived, and offered to draw his sword for the Parliament under the banner of a Prince of the House of Bourbon. The excitement was now so great that Molé requested all the contending chiefs to withdraw, until the magistrates had deliberated on the proposals they had just heard.

While this scene was being enacted in the Palace of Justice, the Coadjutor was busy unfolding the second part of the sensational drama he had so skilfully contrived. Entering the coach of Madame de Longueville, which had conveyed her husband to the Chamber, he carried its fair owner and the Duchess of Bouillon, each dressed with studied negligence and accompanied by her chil-

dren, to the Hotel de Ville, and presented them as
voluntary hostages to the vast multitude that
crowded the Place de Greve. The sight of two
young and beautiful Princesses, holding aloft two
beautiful children, and irresistibly attractive in
the artful disorder of their attire, surrendering
themselves as pledges for the good faith of their
husbands, at the head-quarters of the city, took
the hearts of the Parisians by storm. The men
shouted till they were hoarse; the women wept
for joy, and the popular enthusiasm soon found
an echo in the deliberations at the Palace of
Justice. The majority of the magistrates re-
pented of their engagements with Elbœuf. The
insinuations sown broadcast by the Coadjutor, and
which were not altogether unfounded, had borne
fruit, and seriously damaged the reputation of the
new General. He himself, daunted by the powerful
confederacy so suddenly arrayed against him,
lowered his tone of confident self-assertion, and
evinced a disposition to compromise his claims.
Conti, though imbecile, deformed, and a dwarf,
was a Prince of the Blood, whose rank gave dignity
and strength to opposition. It was clear that by
rejecting him the Parliament would forfeit the
assistance of the territorial magnates, whose military knowledge and provincial influence must avail
much in a prolonged struggle against the Regent,

and would provoke dangerous popular tumults. The perils attending his election were comparatively remote, and might be warded off; the perils attending his rejection were certain and immediate. These considerations more than counterbalanced the arguments of the First President. The High Court, after long deliberation, passed a decree appointing Conti Commander-in-Chief; Elbœuf, Bouillon, and Marshal la Mothe, Generals; Beaufort, Marsillac, and Normoutier, Lieutenant-generals of the armies of the Parliament. Longueville departed for Normandy, to raise troops, leaving his wife, to her intense delight, installed at the Hotel de Ville, ruling with undisputed sway as Queen of the Fronde.

The defection of Conti and Longueville burst like a thunder-clap on Anne of Austria and the Cardinal. It threw Condé into transports of fury. He sought to relieve his feelings by parading a miserable hunchback, sheathed in gilded armour, before the whole Court, as the new Generalissimo of the Fronde; and, by strenuous efforts, to cut off the supplies of the capital, and such of its defenders as their exemplary prudence suffered to come within his reach. But his small army of fourteen thousand men was inadequate to seal up all the avenues of a populous city. Until the expected junction of the army of Germany, under Turenne, he could do no more than occupy the more important posts in the vicinity of Paris, and send detachments of cavalry to scour the adjacent country.

The amazement that seized the minds of the Regent and her crafty minister at the powerful combination, which seemed to have sprung out of the earth to confront them, was the most flattering homage to the creative genius of De Retz. His bold and profound scheming had proved more than a match for the wary subtlety of his rival. The Cardinal trembled at the unforeseen dangers which had risen like a lion in his path, and still more at others more terrible, of which he now discerned the advancing shadows. But Anne of Austria, exasperated to a greater degree than ever against her ancient friends, the Importants, breathed only vengeance. A royal proclamation declared the princes and nobles who should not immediately retire from Paris guilty of high treason. Even this, however, did not check the epidemic of desertion from the Court, and every day saw new and powerful accessions to the insurgent ranks.

The Generals of the Parliament, with the exception of Conti, whose constitutional infirmities unfitted him for warfare, and Bouillon, who held the dignity in contempt, laboured incessantly in drilling and organizing the city levies. The arrival of the Duke of Beaufort and the Prince of Marsillac infused fresh activity into the military preparations. The presence of the former nobleman was especially welcome to the Coadjutor. As he says himself, he wanted a "phantom to hide behind" in his manipulation of the Parisian populace; and he could not possibly have found any one more suitable for his purpose than a grandson of Henry IV., whose gallant bearing and familiar use of their idiom made him the idol of the lower classes, and whose vanity and slender capacity made him a pliant tool. Popularity, even in its sweetest moments, has its penalties. The career of the Duke was well-nigh brought to a premature close, on the day of his return to the Capital, by the too vehement caresses of the ladies of the fish-markets.

Notwithstanding the exertions of their leaders, the operations of the Parliamentary forces were far more fruitful of laughter than of glory or advantage; their martial enthusiasm within the walls being alloyed with a lamentable excess of discretion in the field. The first enterprise undertaken by the Generals was the attack of the Bastille. The Governor, being unprovided with the means of defence, intimated his intention not to offer resistance; but a military spectacle was arranged for the encouragement of the citizen troops. A few cannons, charged with powder, opened fire against the walls. The guns of the fortress thundered in equally harmless defiance. The Duchesses of Longueville and Bouillon, arrayed in habits of blue, the colour of the Fronde, profusely sprinkled with golden slings, came and seated themselves on chairs in the neighbouring gardens of the Arsenal. Surrounded by a sling-spangled body-guard of daring young cavaliers, they exposed themselves freely to danger, within range of the hostile ramparts, and regaled themselves on sweet-meats with cheerful composure. When the garrison had made a sufficiently heroic defence, it capitulated, and marched out with all the honours of war.

A few days after this notable achievement a large body of the citizens sallied forth with great bravery of equipment, under Marshal la Mothe, to seize St. Denis. At their approach, two hundred Swiss Guards advanced from the village. A panic instantly seized the Parisian braves. Without firing a shot, they turned and fled in the wildest confusion, and never halted till they found themselves safe within the city gates. They were received by their fellow citizens with shouts of derision. Lampoons, squibs, caricatures, celebrated their prowess. The exploit of the regi-

ment of the Coadjutor and titular Archbishop of
Corinth, which had borne away the palm in the
race of cowardice, was termed by the irreverent
Parisians "the first of the Corinthians." The
public amusement was heightened by the explanation of the Generals, who announced that their
troops had only retired out of profound respect
for the royal flag. This laudable sentiment long
remained sufficiently powerful to render the civic
cohorts proof against the ridicule of their friends.
Every day one or other of the chiefs led out a
strong force to protect the convoys of provisions
required to feed the Capital. A distant glimpse
of a few of Condé's horsemen usually had the
effect of sending back the doughty champions of
liberty in breathless terror to the city gates ; and
the woeful plight of the burgher exquisites who
had gone forth bedizened with the gaudiest extravagance of military foppery, bruised by falls in
the muddy ditches, and grievously wounded by
the brambles that had impeded their flight,
kindled inextinguishable mirth amongst the
laughter-loving populace. Gaiety reigned supreme,
and pointed its shafts with impartial freedom.
One day at a crowded meeting a dagger was seen
sticking from the pocket of De Retz. "Behold,"
exclaimed the Duke of Beaufort, to the delighted
throng, "the breviary of our Archbishop!" The

cavalry of the city, raised and maintained by the tax on the larger houses, was called the Cavalry of the "*portes cocheres*" and was popularly described as being "More horse than foot, in order the better to run away from the enemy." Every evening the Duchess of Longueville held high festival in the Hotel de Ville. The superb building, shining forth a huge mountain of light, was thronged by all who were distinguished or notorious in the capital. Every variety of the motley Parisian life was represented there. The flower of the high nobility, redolent of the delicate fragrance of the Hotel Rambouillet, or the reeking odours of godless saloons, venerable ecclesiastics, foul-tongued scoffers, dignified presidents of Parliament, vulgar demagogues, fastidious prudes, flaunting courtezans, jostled each other at every step in the overflowing rooms. The ludicrous disasters of the day lent a keener edge to wit, and a more delicious zest to enjoyment. Music and dancing flung around their voluptuous spells, and an occasional council of war, at which the Duchess presided, attested the provident cares of the chiefs. The square outside, packed with a dense multitude, rang with the blare of trumpets, sounded by Conti's orders, to breathe martial fury into the souls of the citizens. This nightly *fanfarronade*, and the daily exertion of conducting a foraging expedition to one of the city gates, and receiving it on its return, comprised the services rendered by the Prince as Commander-in-Chief. The military peals were varied by the more congenial strains of a Mazarinade, or by a stirring harangue delivered by some popular orator from the balcony of the Hotel de Ville.

In the midst of these scenes of grotesque excitement, which lapped her in an elysium of flattered vanity, the political labours of Madame de Longueville were interrupted by her accouchement. But this unseasonable event proved the occasion of her crowning triumph. The day of the child's baptism was observed as a public festival. The rite, administered by the Coadjutor, was surrounded with extraordinary pomp. The City of Paris and the Duchess of Bouillon stood sponsors; the infant, Charles Paris, was borne back from the church in triumphal procession, and then exposed, in a magnificent cradle, on the steps of the Hotel de Ville, to the enthusiastic homage of the rabble.

The ludicrous incidents of the war, however, were varied by sterner episodes, although even these were not without ridiculous features. The village of Charenton, a post of great importance for securing the entrance of supplies into the Capital, had been occupied by three thousand of the flower of the Parisian army, under the command of the Marquis of Clanlieu, a gallant soldier. Condé, seizing with savage joy the opportunity of striking a terrible blow, rushed down upon the village with five thousand foot and three thousand horse. He directed his friend, the Duke of Chatillon, to storm the place with the infantry, while he pushed forward in person, at the head of the cavalry, in the direction of Paris to cover the assault. The garrison, stung by the shame of past disgraces, fought with desperate resolution. Quarter was neither asked nor given. Chatillon and Clanlieu fell at the head of their men in the hottest of the fight; and, after an hour's fearful carnage, Charenton was carried. One insurgent officer, the Marquis of Coignac, escaped by springing on a large fragment of ice, which floated him down the Seine into the city; the rest of the defenders were put to the sword. Blackened heaps of smouldering ruins, thickly strewn with charred corpses, and soaked in blood, alone remained to tell the story of gratified vengeance. Before the attack began, Elbœuf, having received timely intimation of Condé's purpose, assembled twenty thousand of the municipal bands to succour Clanlieu. But the sight of the redoubtable Prince, watching their tardy evolutions at the head of his cavalry, caused the hearts of the citizens to sink within them. De Retz, booted and spurred, a sword at his side and pistols in his holsters, and Madame de Longueville, who, still ailing, had risen from her couch to distribute azure scarves with her own fair hands, vainly essayed to raise their spirits. Honour pricked them on, but discretion held them back. Elbœuf, perplexed and incapable, held a council of war, wherein it was resolved that, considering the impetuous valour of the Parisian troops, an attempt to dislodge the foe must result in the loss of valuable citizens, and the lamentations of their wives. Rather than incur the risk of such calamities, the tenderhearted General sounded a retreat. Clanlieu was abandoned to his fate, and Condé, glutted with slaughter, was left in undisturbed possession of the field.

A few days after the storming of Charenton, the Duke of Beaufort led out a numerous force to protect the return of the Marquis of Noirmoutier, who had collected in the neighbourhood of Paris a large herd of cattle. A train of shrieking amazons from the fish-markets accompanied their hero to the gate, vowing horrible retaliation upon all who should dare to assail him. The insurgents soon came into collision with a body of cavalry under Marshal Grammont. Beaufort fought like a lion, at the head of his men; though wounded and disarmed he gallantly maintained the battle, and after a stiff contest, both sides retired. Some fugitives, however, carried exaggerated rumours of his danger into Paris. Immediately thirty thousand of the lower classes, men, women, and children, armed with spits, brooms, and every homely weapon they could snatch up in haste, rushed forth to the rescue of the King of the Markets. They found him at a considerable distance from the walls quietly awaiting the coming up of the convoy. Transported with joy at his safety, the fish-hags threw themselves upon him in a species of Bacchanalian frenzy, almost stifled him and his horse in their embraces, and then squatting over the adjacent fields watched patiently for several hours, to shield him from further peril. At last Noirmoutier, having luckily eluded the vigilance of Condé's skirmishers, made his appearance; and then, with wild laughter and tears and extravagant gambols, the vast *cortége* returned to Paris, soldiers, populace, and cattle mingled together in inextricable confusion. A charge of the Royal troops must have ended in a fearful massacre.

The ridicule provoked by their inglorious exploits, the grief daily renewed by the spectacle of their damaged finery, the ruin of their trade, the pressure of taxation, the increasing dearth of provisions, soon thoroughly disgusted the substantial burghers with the war. Their feelings were shared by the majority of the Parliament. Abhorring the very name of rebellion, and armed only in legitimate defence of the Declaration of October, Molé and his friends were scared by the tragic fall of royalty in England, and learned with misgiving that their Generals had entered into a secret compact not to disband their troops until the personal demands of each had been fully satisfied. Intelligence of this favourable change of disposition was privately conveyed to Mazarin by the Municipal Authorities, who, though compelled to temporise with the insurrection, had remained staunchly loyal.

The Government, on its side, was urged by the most powerful motives to seek an accommodation. Several of the provincial Parliaments had espoused the quarrel of the Parliament of Paris, and launched Decrees of banishment against the Cardinal. Numerous towns and fortresses throughout the kingdom had declared for the Fronde. The public taxes, diverted from the royal treasury, supplied the Dukes of Longueville, La Tremouille, and other potent insurgent nobles with the means of raising armaments for the relief of the Capital. The greater part of the military force, which the peace of Munster had promised to place at the disposal of the Regent, had either disbanded or mutinied for want of pay, or was dispersed to curb the disaffection of the provinces. The dubious conduct of Viscount Turenne caused serious uneasiness at Court. It was known there that this great General was listening to the solicitations of his brother, to lead back the army of Germany against Condé. It was also known that the Archduke Leopold, eagerly watching his opportunity to extort favourable conditions of peace for exhausted Spain, meditated marching a powerful force over the naked frontier. The investing body was not only insufficient to capture Paris, but was exposed to be overwhelmed by the converging attacks of superior armies. The angry clouds that hurried up in gathering ruin from every point of the political horizon made Cardinal Mazarin tremble for France; the hostile Decrees of so many of the great judicial bodies made him tremble for himself, and in his nightly conferences with his mistress, he was the strenuous advocate of peace. He represented to Anne of Austria that an implacable prosecution of hostilities would arm the Generals and demagogues of the capital with a pretext for crushing the loyal majority of the High Court, or forcing it into an alliance with Spain; would light up throughout the entire kingdom the flames of civil war, and must result

in delivering over the realm as a spoil to its
foreign and domestic enemies, or in rendering
the victorious Condé military dictator during the
minority of her son. On the other hand, a temporary compliance with the demands of Molé
and his party, demands more than once conceded, and which might be again revoked,
would cut the ground from under the
traitorous nobles and re-establish her authority
upon the support of the Parliament. The
prospect of seeing herself and her cherished
minister at the mercy of her discarded friends,
the "Importants," aided by the troops of her
brother, or puppets of the imperious Condé,
was intolerable to Anne of Austria. While she
listened, half convinced, to Mazarin's counsels,
a warning voice, eloquent in all the force of tragic
experience, fell upon her ear. The unhappy
Henrietta Maria, Queen of England, had remained
behind in her cheerless solitude at the Louvre
after the departure of the Court. One day, in
the depth of the unusually severe winter, De
Retz found her without food or fire, shivering by
the bed-side of her daughter, who was unable to
rise on account of the extreme cold. The sight
of a great Queen, the daughter, sister, and aunt of
a King of France, destitute of the necessaries of
life in the principal palace of her royal race,

touched the not ungenerous heart of the Coadjutor, and he obtained for her a liberal provision from the Parliament. Shortly afterwards the news of the judicial murder of her husband plunged the ill-fated lady in anguish and despair. In her desolation she implored her sister-in-law to be wise in time, and to beware of arousing, by arbitrary acts, the ferocious passions of an infuriated people.

The gravity of the situation also sobered Condé, hitherto the fiercest advocate of repression. He felt convinced that he had done enough to command the lasting gratitude of the Regent, who loaded him with marks of affection, constantly styling him her third son; and he was not insensible to the glory of again giving peace to France.

The result of this revulsion of feeling at St. Germain was, that the deliberations of the Coadjutor and his military allies were disturbed by the unwelcome intelligence that a royal herald, bearing letters for the High Court, had presented himself at the city gates and demanded audience. In the present temper of the citizens, the opening of communication between the Court and the Parliament was fraught with ruin to the personal projects of the insurgent leaders. De Retz, ever fertile in resource, hit upon an ingenious mode of averting the danger. He hinted to Broussel that as heralds were sent only to sovereign princes and rebels, the present mission was a perfidious device of Cardinal Mazarin to entrap the Parliament into a confession of high treason. This plausible theory, greedily accepted and confidently expounded by Broussel and his democratic friends, had the expected effect of filling the majority of the magistrates with distrustful fears. But Molé adroitly foiled the Coadjutor with his own weapons. Acquiescing in the validity of the plea against receiving the King's missive, he carried a resolution that the law officers of the Crown should be deputed to St. Germain to explain to the Regent that jealous loyalty and not disrespect prompted the refusal. The Attorney-General, the eloquent and patriotic Omer Talon, and his colleagues, discharged their commission with zeal and prudence. Their excuses were graciously listened to by the Regent. They learned that the royal letter had only exacted the retirement of the Parliament for one day to Montargis, as the price of a general amnesty; and their rose-coloured pictures on their return of the benevolent dispositions of the Court, fostered the growing desire of peace.

A premature agreement between Anne of Austria and the Parliament of Paris, which left Mazarin Prime Minister of France, must topple down the ladder of intrigue which De Retz had constructed with so much secret toil and skill to form his own ascent to power. The time was come when, in order to inspirit his partizans and to baffle the efforts of the peace party, it was necessary for him to play a bolder game; to unmask the deeper and more dangerous operations of his policy, to which the revolt of the Capital was meant to serve as an introduction. The civil war now passed into a graver and sterner phase. The laughable incidents and the gay frivolity, which had given it the character of a glittering comedy, disappeared. The splendid phantoms that had been paraded to attract the popular favour faded away into the background, and the interest centred in the real actors. The jealousy of the Prince of Marsillac had severed the intimate relations of Madame de Longueville with the Coadjutor—and shortly afterwards a dangerous wound, which the Prince received in a sally, bereft her also of his support. Nature had not formed her for the rough career of a revolutionary heroine. The Hotel Rambouillet, with its refined pleasures and its circle of brilliant adorers, was her proper sphere. The timid Conti, still less at ease amidst the rude familiarities and the violent passions of a Parisian mob, instead of being a prop, leant on her for protection. Chagrined and dispirited she retired into privacy; and the Hotel de Bouillon, whither the Coadjutor repaired every day to confer with the Duke and his energetic wife, became the head quarters of the Fronde.

De Retz and Bouillon, by far the ablest men and the most sternly in earnest of the insurgent party, were thoroughly in accord as regarded the policy of overthrowing the existing Government. But their different political views and personal aims caused a divergence of opinion as to the means that should be adopted to accomplish this purpose. Bouillon opposed Cardinal Mazarin as the leading representative of a system which triumphed by his own abasement, and the abasement of his order. He sought to be re-established in his sovereign dignity, and his forfeited territory of Sedan, to aggrandize his family connexions, and, as a more remote object of desire, to restore the feudal power of the nobles. Contemning public rights, other than those of the higher orders of the realm, chafed by the pretensions of the Chambers, and by association with plebeian gownsmen, having no sympathy for the grievances of the Third Estate, he wished to coerce the Parliament and rule the Capital by the terror of organized mobs; to invite the Spanish army of Flanders to co-operate with the troops of Turenne, the provincial levies of the territorial magnates, and the Parisian forces in dictating terms to the Crown.

He had hitherto held himself aloof from active participation in the war, wrapping himself up in haughty isolation until the preparations of the Archduke, of Turenne, and of his aristocratic confederates were sufficiently matured to enable him to assume a position corresponding to his claims. He now proposed to cast aside the cause of the Parliament and the constitution of October as a worn-out garment, to crush the opposition of the loyal magistrates, and, strong in his potent alliances, to confront Anne of Austria as an equal competitor for the possession of France. The other Generals coincided in his views.

De Retz hated Mazarin as a personal rival. Having no longer any hope of supplanting his enemy in the favour of the Regent, he sought to drive him from the kingdom by the force of a popular movement deriving its sanction from the venerable authority of the Parliament, which would bear himself on its crest to the direction of affairs. In order to endue this movement with the power, energy, and prestige necessary to overturn a long-established and successful administration, he had drawn into it discontented ambitions of Princes of the Blood and feudal chiefs, which only partially approved themselves to his convictions; and he even desired the intervention of the Spaniards so far as it could be made subservient to his main object. But it was counter to his views to destroy the authority of the great judicial body which was the chief pillar of his own ambition; which, by countenancing the revolt, raised it from a mere outbreak of faction into a patriotic assertion of national rights, clothed it with the strength of justice and legality, and enlisted in its support the active sympathies of the middle classes. It was equally contrary to his intentions, by any rash step, to place himself beyond the pale of Parliamentary protection, a safe object for the vengeance of the Regent. As wary as he was bold, he was the soul of the rebellion, and yet carefully guarded his own security. He moved all the springs of the Fronde without letting his hand be too conspicuous. Through Beaufort he ruled the populace of Paris. Through Bouillon and the other Generals he guided the military operations and the Spanish intrigues. Through Broussel and other popular demagogues he swayed the deliberations of the Chambers. But while bringing all the moral influences he could command to inflame and extend the civil war, and to shape the action of the Parliament in a course of uncompromising resistance, he protected the magistrates from seditious violence, and regulated his steps by their decisions.

It was clear, however, to both of these experienced leaders, that unless the fainting spirits of the Parisians could be raised by an immediate prospect of external aid, the struggle against the Government must collapse. The great provincial nobles still required time to complete their armaments. Turenne, thwarted by the opposition of Baron d'Erlach, Colonel of the Swiss, had not yet ventured on a public declaration of his intentions. Alliance with Spain would be spurned by the Parliament with horror. But it occurred to the Coadjutor that it might be possible, by a surprise, to trick the High Court into an appearance of friendly communication with the Archduke Leopold, which, by feeding the war fever in the Capital, and by incensing the Regent, must cast new obstacles in the way of an accommodation.

The Archduke had recently accredited a skilful agent to De Retz and Bouillon, a monk named Arnulphini, furnished with a number of blank forms signed by Leopold, and with a formal letter of credence to the Duke of Elbœuf, to be used according as the two leading chiefs might see fit. This envoy, acting in concert with the Coadjutor, now assumed the name and garb of Don Joseph de Illescas, a Spanish cavalier, and presented the letter. Elbœuf, who was vain and presumptuous, received the Archduke's communication as a flattering mark of distinction. With an air of mysterious importance, that was highly diverting to the contrivers of the intrigue, he invited his military colleagues and De Retz to a conference at his hotel, and introduced to them the pseudo ambassador. In the afternoon of the same day, the Prince of Conti announced, from his place in the Chamber, that the Archduke Leopold, having been offered most advantageous terms of peace by Cardinal Mazarin, who wished to have his hands free to oppress the Parliament, had not only refused to abet the designs of the proscribed minister, but had dispatched a special envoy to crave audience of the High Court. The Prince concluded by divulging the arrival of Don Joseph de Illescas, and proposing that he should at once be heard. The motion was listened to by the majority of the Chamber with alarm and indignation. The President de Mesmes, hurried away by patriotic anger, poured a torrent of invective upon the head of the unmoved Coadjutor. In the unguarded rush of his passion, he let fall a phrase which wounded the self-love of the magistrates. De Retz promptly interrupted his assailant, and in a happy retort carried the Chamber so completely with him, that the loyal majority, yielding to the clamour, reluctantly consented to grant the envoy audience.

Arnulphini immediately presented himself, fortified by credentials and letters, which De Retz had manufactured with the help of the Archduke's signatures. He informed the magistrates that his master, out of respect for their illustrious body, the legal depository of the royal authority during the minority of Louis XIV., had declined to countenance Cardinal Mazarin; that the Archduke was ready to treat for peace with France at any place the Parliament should appoint, and in the meantime placed twenty thousand troops at its service. Having finished his harangue, he delivered his letters, and by the order of the First President was conducted from the Chamber. By this time the cloud of passion which obscured the judgment of the assembly had passed away, and been followed by a re-action of patriotic fears. Molé, seeing his advantage, proposed that a deputation should carry the letters to St. Germain, and inform the Regent that the Parliament had not presumed to deliberate on, or even to open them without the royal permission. A decree to this effect passed without opposition, and the Coadjutor found his bold artifice foiled, a second time, by the calm decision of the First President.

The failure of this clever imposture exasperated the Generals. Bouillon urged the Coadjutor to excite a popular commotion, to arrest, and imprison

Molé, and the principal men of the hostile party, and to join in a letter demanding armed assistance from the King of Spain. But De Retz, knowing that the Spanish alliance was the rock upon which the most powerful confederacies against Richelieu had foundered, and that the destruction of the independence of the Parliament would be the shipwreck of his own fortunes, resolutely refused his assent. "All things," he said, "with the Parliament; nothing without it." The Generals, therefore, were obliged to restrict themselves to negotiating with the Court of Brussels, on their own responsibility, and to sending pressing messages to their provincial allies to hasten their movements.

The Coadjutor's stratagem, though baffled in the Chamber, was not without its effect at St. Germain. Anne of Austria, irritated by the public audience granted to her brother's envoy, listened to the explanations and excuses of Molé and his colleagues with impatience. The entreaties of the First President, seconded by the advice of Orleans, Condé, and Mazarin, wrung from her with difficulty a peevish consent to a conference, in which terms of agreement might be discussed. She privately made it an absolute condition that the Cardinal's position of Prime Minister should not be questioned. On the other hand, she promised to allow a daily supply of provisions to enter the Capital, where the populace, pinched by the approaches of famine, showed a disposition to repeat the revolutionary excesses of their fathers in the days of Bussy le Clerc and the "Sixteen." Armed with this concession, the First President returned to Paris, and treating with calm scorn the ferocious threats of the dregs of the population, who were subsidised by Bouillon, persuaded the High Court to accept the conference. The Generals again proposed to assassinate or seize him, and to kindle an insurrection ; and again De Retz steadily withstood their pressure, and the more dangerous assaults of the Duchess of Bouillon.

The presidents Viole and Coigneux, leaders of the extreme party, were associated with Molé and De Mesmes to represent the Chamber at Ruel, the seat of the negotiations. The principal members of the Council of State attended on behalf of the Crown. But the conditions insisted on by the Regent were found to be as haughty and severe as if she were imposing the harsh law of the conqueror on prostrate rebels. They exacted the exile of the High Court to Montargis, and the suppression or curtailment of its newly acquired privileges. It was impossible for the magistrates to accept a humiliation which involved the surrender of the principles embodied in the Declaration of October. But Anne of Austria, jealous of the dignity of the Crown, and submitting with ill-humour to the temporising policy of her Council, could not be induced to relax her demands. The negotiations came to a dead-lock, and after many days of barren discussion it seemed as if the conference was about to terminate without result.

While the delegates were wasting their hours in fruitless debates, the course of events had wrought a complete change in the character and prospects of the Civil War and in the temper of the Capital. Turenne, crossing the Rhine at the head of his army, had issued a proclamation in which he assumed the title of Lieutenant-General of the King's army in the service of the Parliament, and had set out on his march for Paris. Before the citizens recovered from the first fever of joyful excitement into which this news had thrown them, messengers from Normandy announced the advance of the Duke of Longueville, with ten thousand men, on St. Germain, to capture the King and the Regent. Fast upon the heels of Longueville's couriers came others from the south to herald the arrival of a still more numerous force under the Duke of La Tremouille. A second agent, despatched by the Archduke Leopold, having concluded a secret treaty with the Generals, the enterprising Marquis of Noirmoutier had departed for Brussels to hasten the invasion of the Spaniards. And in order better to co-operate with the movements of his allies, Bouillon led out fourteen thousand of the best of the Parisian troops to an entrenched camp at Villejuif, in the angle formed by the junction of the Seine and Marne—a position which Condé pronounced to be unassailable. The agitation of the populace rose to frenzy. The inflexible severity of the Regent, and the toleration extended to Cardinal Mazarin, alienated the middle classes. The party of the Coadjutor obtained the upper hand in the Chambers, and the Parliament resolved, by a large majority, to cancel the powers of its delegates, and recall them from Ruel.

The intelligence that reached him from the Capital filled the patriotic heart of Molé with grief for the calamities impending over the monarchy. An intercepted copy of the treaty concluded by Bouillon and his colleagues with the King of Spain, which was communicated to him by the Regent, excited in his breast poignant feelings of shame and indignation. He had, up to this time, scrupulously avoided any recognition of Cardinal Mazarin's presence at Ruel, but now all other considerations were lost in an over-mastering purpose to save the State from the machinations of traitors.

With his friend De Mesmes, who shared his views, he repaired at midnight to Mazarin's lodgings, and told the astonished Minister that, having received intimation that their commission would be revoked on the following day, they were prepared to risk their lives, and sign without further delay any treaty which he might dictate. It was for the Ministers' interest to grant such conditions as would justify their act to the Parliament, and enable them to defeat the practices of the confederate lords; but, whatever he might determine, their part was chosen. Mazarin, fully appreciating the peril of the situation and the magnanimity of the magistrates, summoned Orleans and Condé, and wrote out the draft of a new treaty. In whatever touched the dignity of the Crown this document was studiously exacting; but the concessions were as large as he could hope to extort from the Regent. The banishment of the Parliament to Montargis was commuted to a visit to St. Germain; its political discussions were subjected to a temporary restraint; the Government reserved to itself the right of borrowing money for its present necessities; but the Declaration of October the 24th was explicitly confirmed, and a general amnesty was guaranteed. With the draft in his pocket, the Cardinal started off for St. Germain, and after some hours returned with it, signed by

the Regent. Molé and De Mesmes wept for joy
—and even Coigneux and Viole, scared by the
Spanish treaty, affixed their names without hesitation. The signatures were scarcely dry when
messengers arrived with the decree of the High
Court annulling the powers of its representatives.
Molé displayed the treaty in triumph, and returned
to Paris, amidst the hootings and execrations of
the rabble, conscious of his danger, and prepared
to devote his life for his country.

The Parliament, though strongly adverse to a
compromise with the Regent, which left Cardinal
Mazarin at the helm of affairs, had adjourned in
order to give its First President a hearing before
coming to a decision. The Generals were determined to use all means to prevent the ratification
of the treaty. At an early hour of the morning
Paris exhibited all the signs of feverish agitation.
The seditious cries and the lowering looks of the
groups, restlessly forming and dissolving in the
places of public resort, gave ominous presage of a
political tempest. At seven o'clock the members
of the High Court were in their places, and Molé
read out the minutes of the proceedings at Ruel.
The reading was frequently interrupted by angry
cries and insolent comments, which swelled at its
conclusion into a tumult of frantic denunciation.
Conti rose, and in gentle tones reproached the

First President with perfidiously betraying the interests of the Generals, who were abandoned by the treaty to the vengeance of the outlawed Minister. Bouillon followed, saying curtly, that all he asked of the Chamber was a passport to quit the kingdom, since Mazarin was to be reestablished in his abuse of the royal authority. The deafening clamour and the wild gesticulations which applauded this artful speech had only partially subsided, when a muffled roar, making itself audible above the din, announced the presence of an excited multitude in the Place de Greve. Conti, rising again, repeated his complaints against the First President for concluding a peace without his participation. Then Molé, unable longer to restrain his indignation, started to his feet with flashing eyes, and in a voice of thunder, which subdued the uproar, and arrested universal attention, addressed the Prince—"What, Sir," he exclaimed, " you ask why we concluded peace without your participation ? We did so to circumvent the pernicious, traitorous, and murderous designs of yourself and your colleagues. While we were at Ruel," he continued, turning to the assembly, "our self-styled protectors were negociating with the enemies of France. You," he said to Conti and Bouillon, " sent the Marquis of Noirmoutier to the Archduke. Your letters, which we have read, summoned the Archduke to France, and delivered this fair realm to the ravages of a foreign enemy. You give us such allies without our consent. Can you wonder that we repudiate and resent such an indignity?" The Chamber listened spell-bound in incredulous amazement. "We took this step," faltered the disconcerted Conti, with white lips, " by the advice of certain members of this august Court." "Name them, name them," thundered Molé, "and we will arraign and sentence them as criminals guilty of high treason." His vehement words were echoed back by a storm of applause. The magistrates, revolting from their position of dishonoured dupes, gave free rein to their patriotic resentment. The treaty was about to be voted by acclamation, when a wild clamour of shrieks and yells resounded from the outer hall, and the terrified ushers, rushing into the Chamber, implored the Duke of Beaufort to come forth and address the mob. Armed ruffians, in Bouillon's pay, led on by a lawyer named Deboisle, had invaded the Palace of Justice, loudly demanding Molé's head.

Beaufort was instantly surrounded by a band of viragoes, bereft, by a life of lawless depravity, of all but the form of their sex, who insisted on tearing the First President limb from limb. While he held these furious women in

parley, the multitude behind burst open the side
doors, and with horrible imprecations rushed into
the galleries of the Chamber. Part of the balustrade, yielding to the pressure of the crowd,
crashed down upon the trembling magistrates,
and increased their terror and confusion. Molé
alone remained calm and undaunted. "Never,"
says De Retz, " did I behold such sublime intrepidity as was displayed by M. Molé. Not a
feature quivered, and he exhibited indomitable
firmness, and presence of mind almost supernatural." The members gathered round their
President, and implored him to quit the building
by a door behind the throne, which gave access
to his official residence. " The Court never hides
itself," he replied. " If I knew that my death
was certain, nothing should induce me to fly.
Would not treason be encouraged ? Would not
the rabble seek me in my own house, if I was
guilty of such cowardice?" And he strode forward
proudly towards the grand entrance. De Retz,
moved by generous admiration, threw himself in
the President's path, and besought him at least to
wait until he endeavoured to disperse the rioters.
" Then, my good lord," said Molé, in bitter scorn,
" speak the merciful word quickly." The Coadjutor, disregarding the injurious insinuation which,
in the present instance, was undeserved, mounted

on a bench and harangued the rabble, but was answered with jeers and laughter, and discharges of musketry. He then went to seek Deboisle. Molé, disdaining even the appearance of hesitation, refused to tarry longer, and advanced with a few faithful friends to the head of the principal stair-case. De Retz flew to his side, and Bouillon, ashamed and alarmed at the excesses of his partizans, followed the Archbishop's example. The mob, drunk with fury, set upon them with indiscriminating violence. Bouillon was felled to the ground and trampled under foot by his own adherents. De Retz, in warding off a dagger-thrust from the President's breast, was wounded in the hand. A ruffian put a loaded musket to Molé's head. "When you have killed me," said the illustrious magistrate, with unflinching composure, "I shall only need six feet of earth!" His undaunted bearing and noble presence struck even the frenzied wretches, who thirsted for his blood, with awe. Despite themselves, they allowed him to descend the steps; his friends placed him in the carriage of one of the Generals, and he reached his house in safety.

Early on the following morning Molé was again in his place, with the treaty of Ruel in his hand. The terrible scene of the previous day had left a vivid impression of horror on the minds, even of his opponents in the Chamber. Conti, under whose superior rank his colleagues had sheltered themselves, sick from fright, was unable to leave his bed. The other Generals earnestly deprecated a renewal of mob violence, and declared their desire to use only the weapons of legitimate argument; and the Provost of Paris mustered the Burgher Guard to protect the deliberations of the High Court. In an able speech, Bouillon vaunted the overwhelming military strength of the confederacy, pledged himself to raise the siege of Paris, and to expel Mazarin from France. But the alarm inspired by the Spanish treaty lent irresistible weight to the eloquence of Molé. The Chamber struck out the humiliating clause which imposed on it a penitential journey to St. Germain, and whatever else infringed the rights conceded by the Declaration of October, but accepted the remainder of the treaty by a large majority. The First President was again deputed to obtain the Regent's assent to the required modifications.

No intelligence from Viscount Turenne had reached Paris for several days. The uncertainty that rested on his movements determined the military chiefs not to throw away an opportunity of serving their interests by peaceful negotiations with the Regent; accordingly they sent, through Molé, a formidable schedule of demands for themselves and their friends. Anne of Austria glanced scornfully over this huge catalogue of exactions, which implied a complete change in the distribution of political power, and then threw it aside, as if for future consideration. But a third envoy from the Archduke arriving with intelligence that ten thousand Spaniards had entered Champagne, the Generals resumed their defiant attitude; the High Court again resounded with denunciations of Cardinal Mazarin; and his imputed vices were publicly scourged in fresh lampoons impregnated to the highest point with virulence and wit. The renewed confidence of the war party was unexpectedly dashed, however, by a piece of news which reached the Hotel Bouillon while De Retz and the Spanish envoy were dining, in high spirits, with the Duke and Duchess.

When Turenne's ambiguous proceedings first awakened the suspicions of the Government, the Cardinal had secretly sent a large sum of money and the commission of General to the Baron d'Erlach, with instructions to frustrate any treasonable practices on the part of his superior officer, by discharging the arrears of pay due to the troops, and assuming the supreme command. These precautionary measures proved the salvation of the Government. The army, which was mainly composed of German mercenaries, won over by the

golden arguments of d'Erlach, declared, after a few
marches on the French territory, for the Regent
and Condé. Turenne, abandoned by all except a
few personal attendants, narrowly escaped arrest by
a precipitate flight into Germany. The Spanish
force ravaging Champagne, on hearing of this
defection, beat a rapid retreat into Flanders.

The game of the Fronde was evidently played
out for the present. Baffled and isolated, the
confederate lords were under the necessity of
acquiescing, with what grace they might, in the
restoration of tranquillity. Bouillon, in announcing
to the Parliament the failure of his hopes, declared,
with some dignity, on behalf of the Generals, that
their demands upon the crown were prompted by
the necessity of protecting themselves against
Cardinal Mazarin, and that they were ready to
relinquish all personal claims, if the banished
minister retired from France. · Notwithstanding
this show of disinterestedness, the Cardinal found
them all eager to engage in his favourite political
game of secret intrigue and corruption. He
carried on a separate negotiation with Conti and
Madame de Longueville, with Bouillon, and with
Madame de Montbazon, who still, in spite of time
and absence, reigned without a rival over the
heart of the Duke of Beaufort. The noble
character and devoted loyalty of Molé gave just

weight to his counsels, and he succeeded in persuading the Regent to ratify the treaty of Ruel, as modified by the Parliament. The leaders of the feudal party availed themselves of the amnesty, and, with the exception of Beaufort, presented themselves at court to make their submission. Out of consideration for Condé, Conti obtained the stronghold of Damvilliers in his Government of Champagne, with Marsillac for Lieutenant, enjoying the emoluments; and Longueville was promised possession of Pont de l'Arche, the key of Normandy. Bouillon, the most dangerous conspirator and the deepest in guilt, had to content himself with a vague assurance that his claims would be examined at some future time. Madame de Montbazon, whose greed was insatiable in ministering to her luxurious pleasures, was propitiated by the gift of a large sum of money ; and some favours were conferred on Noirmoutier and other staunch partizans of De Retz. The Coadjutor shaped his own course with his usual judgment. The prudence and foresight which had preserved him from the formal guilt of high treason, saved him now from the humiliation of a public act of submission. He retired to the privacy of his palace, with the declared intention of occupying himself exclusively with his episcopal duties ; and although he sent to the Regent loyal assurances of his unalterable devotion, he declined to visit the Court, or in any way to recognise Mazarin as Prime Minister. By this line of conduct he maintained his credit with the Parisians, and avoided compromising his political aims.

In the beginning of April peace was proclaimed in the Capital; the armies of the Fronde were disbanded; and affairs appeared to resume their normal condition. But the fierce animosities from which the conflict had sprung, and those which it had engendered, though smothered, were scarcely allayed. Society was still agitated by the after-swell of the revolutionary storm. Anne of Austria, mortified at the failure of her policy, distrustful of the temper of the citizens, and deeply galled by the insults and the defiance so freely flung at herself and her cherished minister, refused to enter the impenitent city, and swept by it with her whole Court to pass the summer at Compiegne.

END OF VOL. I.